# TASTE THE COLOUR

# SMELL THE NUMBER

THOUGHTS AND REFLECTIONS
TO
PROVOKE A DEEPER SPIRITUAL WALK WITH GOD

## Acknowledgements

I would like to thank my daughter, Janika Mobley, for her contribution of the five articles about Trees in the Orchard.
I would also like to thank my husband, John, and a friend, Steve Beard, for the contributions they have made to this book.

Introduction

For many years I posted my thoughts and reflections to a Blogging site on the web.  With encouragement from others, who appreciated what they read, I have now added to those articles and turned them into a book.
My desire is to enable us to think and reflect beyond where we have thought before and to provoke a deeper spirituality in our personal and unique journey with God.
I have presented the book in the form of a daily meditation to be read slowly with time spent on each thought letting God bring revelation and deeper insight by His Spirit.

## Taste the colour; Smell the number

The words from a song say - Can you smell the colour 9?
It's not rational;   it's not reasonable
and it doesn't make sense.
But …… Can you smell the colour 9?
It's out there beyond our understanding.
But …… as it stirs my spirit,
as it causes me to cry out "Yes!"
then I know that if God wants me to,
I will…
……. smell the colour 9
for all things are possible with God.
And as I say "Yes" to that statement,
I believe I open myself up to hear
whatever God would want to speak to me.
I don't have to understand it with my mind.
It doesn't have to make sense to me today.
But I want to connect with God's wisdom;
God's knowledge; and God's understanding
I want to catch the wisdom of God in my spirit.
Not to reduce it to the confines of my mind
but to break out from the mind of man
and to explore things I haven't even contemplated;
things I never knew even existed.
For God's thoughts are far out there
And that's where I want to be

## Don't be limited

Don't be limited by the restrictions of the natural world

but let your belief and expectation be rooted

in the nature of God.

The God who can make a universe out of nothing;

The God who sends Gideon with 300 men

to fight against 3,000 and more and to win.

(see Judges 7)

The One who heals on the Sabbath

and who breaks the chains of death.

He still wants to do the unbelievable and unexpected

in people's lives today

but we so often say "No thank you"

when it doesn't fit our mindset,

our logic or our rational thinking!

So ....... Can you smell the colour nine?

Or will your logic even refuse to consider the possibility.

## Mystery

Mystery is not the absence of meaning

but …………..

The presence of more meaning than we can understand.

And that is why God is a mystery to us.

He is more than we can understand.

# A Life Worthwhile

We easily entertain the thought ......
Is my life worthwhile?
We are brought up to ensure that our life is worthwhile;
either in God's purposes or in achieving our own goals.
But that is looking from a wrong perspective ....
and it causes us to be driven people.
Driven to prove that our life is productive, useful, and achieving.
But it's God's life and He created us for His purposes.
To use us <u>where</u> He wants to in outworking His eternal plan.
To use us <u>when</u> He wants to in outworking His eternal plan.
We're in the hands of God and perpetual motion isn't necessary.
We don't have to justify our reason for living.
We need to settle into His plans, to rest in His purposes.
It's not about joining up to a church and its many activities.
It's about daily living kingdom life, with kingdom values
and godly responses to every person and every situation.
It's about a living relationship
and being conformed into His likeness
through our daily situations.
It's about reflecting His character of grace;
humility; meekness and kindness
Not self-seeking and demanding our rights or fair treatment,
but seeking to serve sacrificially as Jesus did.
Seek to know His plan;His eternal plan;
His season of the moment and  know where you fit into that
out of a living relationship with Him

## Vision

If I have no vision then I am going, just going.

Don't know why; don't know where, just going.

Going here; going there; going nowhere in particular;

being taken this way and that by every new idea;

blown by the wind with no direction or purpose.


But with a vision I have set my rudder in a certain direction.

I have purpose and structure.

I know which paths to take and which paths to leave.

I am not distracted by other possibilities

but focused on those things that fit my vision.

So ….. my walk is purposeful and constructive

and I can see fruit because ……

I know what fruit I am looking for.

<u>Do you know your reason for living?</u>

I know I have been sent from heaven

to do a work here…..

before eventually

returning to heaven.

So ….

I need to keep in regular contact

with home base – where God is and

I need to refer back to the Head for …..

mission; assignments;

and on-going instructions.

For wisdom and knowledge in situations.

For relationship with Him and for spiritual sustenance.

I'm on a mission from elsewhere

and I need to keep in touch.

<u>What message do I carry?</u>

The Message I carry

which is downloaded from heaven ……….

to earth is

to know this is a season

where God is outworking

His final purposes.

It is no longer a season for man,

but a season of God.

We are a people preparing the Way

for the return of Jesus.

We are knowing Jerusalem

not Babylon.

We are living Kingdom

not church.

## God's Opportunities or Life's Obstacles?

Do we see opportunities or obstacles in life ?

Do we see adventure or problems ?

The answer is rooted in our knowledge of the Father.

If I really know Him and have reality of relationship

then whatever He sends my way is an adventure

and an opportunity from Him.

If I see it as a problem of the here and now it is rooted in

self-awareness and not God-awareness.

My understanding is rooted in the reasoning of the natural world

not the faith and promises of the spiritual world

and I am not seeing things from His perspective.

I am like the Israelite spies in the promised land

who see the local people as giants

and themselves as grasshoppers;

whereas Joshua and Caleb had eyes to see

the promises of God in the

richness and fruitfulness of the land.

(see Numbers 13)

## Where are you living ?

In The Message Bible Jesus says in John 8
*"You're tied down to the mundane.*
*I'm in touch with what is beyond your horizons.*
*You live in terms of what you can see and touch.*
*I'm living on other terms."*


Can He lay that accusation at my door?
Can He lay it at your door?
Is the physical world superior to the spiritual world
in your thinking?
Whatever we might think or feel
the truth is ....
that the spiritual is superior to the physical.
Whether from the darkness of the enemy
or from the light of God
the spiritual world influences the physical world.
It is the eyes of faith that let us see into the spiritual world,
which is why Paul prays for the Ephesians in 1:18
that the eyes of their hearts would be enlightened,
that they might see more sharply the reality of the spiritual
things.
It should be our constant prayer ......
that the eyes of our heart would be enlightened.
Without eyes of faith we are tied down to the mundane.
With eyes of faith we see beyond the natural horizons
to the works of God in the heavenlies,
and that is what will strengthen our hearts
in the tough times of life.

## Pathways to God

It's my belief that we sometimes get stuck on how we expect to hear God and that is sometimes because we expect to hear Him in the same way as other people do.


But let me suggest that we open ourselves up
to other creative and diverse avenues


For example let me share how I unexpectedly heard from God
just the other day


First, I was provoked by a picture which was a reflection of the word "prophecy."
It showed a man, like a prophet from the Old Testament,
holding back a curtain.
On the curtain were trees and hills
and the curtain being held back suggested
that prophecy is out there beyond the tangible world
beyond our natural horizons.
I desired to see what was beyond the curtain
and sensed in my spirit a picture of a large group of people
seated round a banqueting table – feasting.

This led me to look up the relevant verses in the Bible that speak

of feasting and the abundance of His table.

I wrote two of the verses into my journal

for they seemed to carry something for me.

I wrote them in the first person receiving them into myself

and as I finished writing them I felt more words coming to me.

As I continued to write, I was receiving a

personal word from God into my life.

Encouraging and exciting!


But can you see the steps and the pathway involved?

Beginning with a simple picture

and finishing with a personal word into my life.

God is different for each of us and different each time.

He wants to surprise us and to be found in unexpected places,

like a phrase in a novel or a line in a film.

Be open to finding Him wherever He wants to show Himself.

For those who seek Him will be found by Him,

but not necessarily where we expected.

## How do we Judge?

In The Message Bible Jesus says in John 8
*"You decide according to what you can see and touch.
I don't make judgements like that.
But even if I did My judgement would be true because ....
I wouldn't make it out of the narrowness of my experience
but in the largeness of the One who sent Me, the Father"*

What a statement –
Making judgements out of the narrowness of our experience!
and we think we have something to offer - how futile.
In reality we should be making all judgements out of the
largeness of the One who saves us.
Why? Because God's most foolish thoughts and wisdom
exceed even the best thoughts of men.
(see 1 Corinthians 1:25)
His storehouses are unlimited and beyond comprehension.
Yet we choose so often to tap into our puny little minds.
Know the things that are available out of the relationship we
have with God and access the greatest mind there is,
and surprise yourself.
But remember, God wants fellowship with us and He wants to
keep us close.
That is why His answer to today's problem
won't be the same answer for tomorrow's problem
even if the problem is the same.
God doesn't give us a formula or a method.
He gives us fresh and new every time,
so that we keep coming back to Him
and never stray too far from Him

## Faith

My Master said "Go"

and so I went,

with faith my only friend.

But as I went, I found that faith

could never go alone.

For out of seeds sown in my heart,

grew up a solid tree,

which spread out branches, wide and strong,

so others could go with me.

"Whence came this tree?"

I asked myself

"I did not see it grow!"

My Master must have fed and watered it.

But how, I do not know

## He looks down and sees us

Psalm 33:13 says
*The Lord looks down from Heaven*
*and sees the whole human race.*
*From His throne*
*He observes all who live on the earth.*
*He made their hearts*
*so He understands everything they do.*

How personal is that? He made not just you generally,
but …… He made your heart.
He formed it and fashioned it in His own hand
and He still seeks to hold it in His hand.
He wants to shape it; restore it; heal it; and protect it
because He understands everything we do.
He understands why we react like we do
He understands why we respond like we do.
He knows us better than we know ourselves.
He knows when what seems good is done from wrong motives.
He knows when what seems wrong was done with right motives.
He is seeking to bring us back into His image.
As when He first thought of creating man and said
"Let us make him in our image."
Where that image has been lost by sin
and the circumstances of life
He wants to restore the original form,
for His glory and the honour of His name.
So rest in His hand and be at peace.
Respond to His pathway and be renewed.

20

<u>Righteous before God</u>

Colossians 1:22 (New Living Translation) says
*As a result (of the cross) He has brought you into the very
presence of God, and you are holy and blameless
as you stand before Him
without a single fault.*

How exciting is that !! You stand in God's presence
without a single fault.
So, we don't need to beat ourselves up about things;
we don't need to feel condemned or unworthy.
If we have confessed where we have sinned
and asked His forgiveness
then we can walk tall;
walk confident in this world,
knowing that God allows us to stand in His presence
and that He sees us without a single fault.
Thank you Jesus.

Don't be oppressed or condemned by a lie of the enemy.

Walk tall in the truth - big time !

## Exploring and Discovering

I read the phrase  ......
"the human life should be a constant pilgrimage of discovery"

Yes! my spirit said, I want endless discoveries in God.
We may think the world knows a lot.
Information seems endless.
But compared to the storehouses of God's
wisdom, understanding and knowledge
the knowledge of the world is like a drop in the ocean.
We need to stir ourselves so that we never settle,
so that we are never content,
but always to be hungry and thirsty for more of God.
Thirsty for discovering new things from the heavenly realms.
And know this -
that a whole lifetime of exploring
will only scratch the surface of what we can know with God.
So..... don't hold back through fear of coming to the end of it.
Renew your excitement and anticipation
and discover things that you've never known before.
Discover things that others have never known before.
Believe God when He says in Jeremiah 33:3
*Call unto Me and I will answer you*
*and tell you great and unsearchable things you do not know.*
Believe it, try it, cry out to God
and hear Him answer.

## Saved from .......

1 Peter 3 in The Message Bible says that

Noah and his family were saved from the water

by the water.

Yes .....

They were saved from what they feared

by the very thing they were fearing.

How often will God do that in our lives?

Save us from the thing that is a problem by using that very thing

as the tool!

Consider its application in your life and see where it takes you.

## Day and Night

Psalm 42:8 says

*The Lord will command His loving-kindness*
*concerning me in the day*
*and at night He will sing His songs over me !!*


Yes, it's good to be in fellowship with God during the day
and to be connected with Him in our activities.
But …. how rich to know that we can tune in to the songs
that He sings over us in the night.
If we consciously connect with Him before sleeping
and tune our spirits in to hear His songs
what richness will there be in the night hours!!
Our spirits being nurtured and refreshed,
so that they are not empty hours
but fruitful times for our spirit to grow.


Peaceful night hours and constant fellowship with God!

## What is a Christian?

Am I English because .......
I know the National Anthem?
I support my local football team?
I know the history of the country?
I know the laws of the land?
I understand the economy?
I vote at every election?

No ... I am English because my parents are English
I was born here, and I live here.

So am I a Christian because .....
I read my Bible, and I pray?
I know the theology?
My doctrines are sound?
I believe in all the right things?

No ...... being a Christian is not a philosophy,
a concept, a religion, or a set of beliefs

It is because of a dynamic radical relationship
with a living God;
And being born into His family;
and living in His kingdom.
It's life and lifestyle and relationship
and it affects every level of our existence.

Live the relationship and everything falls into place

<u>Peace and stillness</u>

When you think of peace
which picture is a truer reflection of your understanding......

A peaceful quiet landscape
with lakes and woods and trees
birds singing, and the quiet flow of water?

or

A raging rushing waterfall tumbling over the rocks
with the branch of a birch tree leaning out over the torrent
and a small bird nesting in one of its branches?

It's likely we would pick the first picture, serene and quiet,
but that suggests that we only find peace
when our circumstances are good

True peace is reflected in the second picture.
When ....... all around is raging.
When there is noise and turmoil.
But we can be still and at peace
because it is in our inner being
not in our circumstances.

<u>When the rubber hits the road</u>

So, what happens when the rubber hits the road?

When the pressure is on how do you react ?

With worldly values or kingdom values?


Consider your own situation.

Who irritates you most at home?

Who winds you up at work?

These are the telling situations.

Do you respond with grace and mercy?

Or do they get a tongue lashing?
Do you give peace when they give trial?
Do you give unconditional forgiveness when they give offence?
Do you change the atmosphere or worsen the atmosphere?
These are the gauges that show how much we are still living from
the flesh and how much we are living from the Spirit.
But it's not for condemnation,
it's for freedom.
We can't change ourselves by self effort.
But we can acknowledge to God
that we are willing to let Him do the work that is needed
to make us more like Christ and then watch Him do it.

## How do we handle suffering?

I was considering how some people turn away from God or rage at Him when affliction comes into their lives or into the lives of their loved ones and they demand answers or reasons for the situation. I thought how although God may not send the affliction it is an indicator to Him and ourselves what is truly in our hearts.  It exposes what is really there.

*The heart is deceitful above all things and beyond cure.*

*Who can understand it?*  Jer 17:9

When Jesus suffered at the hands of men from injustice and criticism during His life but more particularly the pain and suffering in His death – for both God and Jesus it is an example to us as to what was and is in their heart - love and grace no matter what the depth of pain.

Jesus, when He was suffering, continued to love us; spoke out forgiveness for the soldiers; ministered life and truth to the dying thief; and showed care and compassion for His mother and John. All this while He was actually hanging on the cross! Not sitting in some easy situation feeling very holy and humble, but being persecuted and crucified!

And God, in His own time of suffering, seeing His Son dying for us sinners continued to love us. He loved us even though, the Israelites in particular, had regularly turned against Him to other gods and sinned against Him in all ways possible. He was willing to live through the pain of it all because of His eternal love for us. No matter what the pain or what the pressure, you can only squeeze goodness out of the heart of God. No matter how deep you go into the hidden depths you can only find love.

But what is found in the hidden depths of our hearts, buried deep so that even we have deceived ourselves as to what is there. When we are struggling or suffering we shouldn't be blaming or questioning the circumstances but we should be willing to take stock and see the reality of what it is exposing in us and deal with that if it is not as pure as it should be.

Gen 6:5 tells us - *The Lord saw how great man's wickedness on the earth had become, and that every inclination of the thoughts of his heart was only evil all the time.*

And Jer 16:*12 But you have behaved more wickedly than your fathers. See how each of you is following the stubbornness of his evil heart instead of obeying me.*

And Heb 3:12 *See to it, brothers, that none of you has a sinful, unbelieving heart that turns away from the living God.*

## How did Jesus come?

Why did Jesus seem to break all the rules?

He touched lepers;

He healed on the Sabbath;

He forgave sins;

He didn't wash His hands before eating;

He let His disciples pick corn on the Sabbath;

He spoke to women even a Samaritan woman;

And many other issues that we read in the Gospels.

He was challenging the spirit and the heart of the people,

not the rules of the book.

Do we live in freedom?

Do we live from the spirit?

Or do we live in bondage to rules and laws?

If there is any bondage in your life,

get free of it and

live in the freedom that Jesus gained for you

on the cross.

## Did He really mean it? (1)

Did Jesus really mean it when He said in Matt 23:8-10

*But you are not to be called 'Rabbi', for you have only one Master*
*and you are all brothers.*
*And do not call anyone on earth 'father', for you have one Father,*
*and He is in heaven.*
*Nor are you to be called 'teacher', for you have one Teacher, the*
*Christ.*

And to this list we could presumably add "Pastor, Minister,
Reverend"

So, did He really mean it or was He just wasting words?

So if He really meant it why do so many people disregard it as if it
is of no consequence?

## Did He really mean it? (2)

Did Jesus really mean it when He said in Luke 6:30

*Give to everyone who asks you,*
*and if anyone takes what belongs to you,*
*do not demand it back.*

Did He really mean for us to live by this principle or
was He just wasting words?

Why then, do so few of us live by what He says?
Rather, we choose
who we will give to and who we won't;
who we will lend to and who we won't,
and these choices are generally based on past experience of

a) how much do they ask of us more often than we want to give?
b) if we lend it will they give it back and in good condition?
c) have they got character issues in these areas
that need working on and I'll be the one to teach them?

Jesus gives no exclusion clauses, He just says do it!

Are we living different to the world?
With faith if we do what seems outrageous to our common sense
we will, in fact, invest richly into our eternal bank account

## Did He really mean it ? (3)

Did Jesus really mean it when He said in Luke 6:35-36

*But love your enemies, do good to them,*
*and lend to them without expecting to get anything back.*
*Then your reward will be great, and you will be sons of the Most*
*High,*
*because He is kind to the ungrateful and wicked.*
*Be merciful, just as your Father is merciful.*

If He asks us to show such love and mercy to our enemies
how much more should we show grace and mercy to those
around -  family; workmates; neighbours
those we come into contact with in our daily routine?

Do we still have the values of the world where we expect
fairness; justice; to be understood; to speak our mind?
Or do we live the values of the kingdom
willing to suffer injustice; to be slighted by others;
to be taken advantage of etc.
It goes against the flesh?
It doesn't have temporal rewards.
But it does have eternal rewards
and we need to have eyes that see the eternal.
Jesus walked the way of the undemanding;
overlooked; offended; misunderstood and set the example for us

# The example of Jesus

John 12:6 says
*He (Judas) did not say this because he cared about the poor*
*but because he was a thief;*
*as keeper of the money bag,*
*he used to help himself to what was put into it.*

Jesus knew that Judas was a thief and stealing from the money
bag.
But what did Jesus do?
Did he remove this responsibility from Judas
knowing that he was stealing from the funds?
Seemingly not.

And what did he do when he went to the wedding at Cana?
The people had already had plenty to drink
but were looking for and expecting more!
Did Jesus say they had already had plenty and leave them short?
Seemingly not.

Yet ......
What would we do to the church treasurer that was stealing
from the offering?
What would we do to a group of people
who were already drunk but asking for more?

This is the real challenge to our value system.
God's values don't sit well with our mind or our flesh.
But God knows best and we have to walk in faith and trust
when we choose to walk His way

In choosing to walk our own way in life
such as walking away from a marriage when it doesn't suit our
flesh anymore
even though this is wholly acceptable by our present culture.
Where has it left us?
What has the breakdown of family life
done to the whole of society?
Maybe God did know best when He expected us to remain
together  "til death do us part"
(see Romans 7:2-3)

And with that as an example we can believe that all other worldly
values, that are different to God's,
lead to death and destruction in the soul.
Whereas God wants to restore our soul
to give abundant life and an eternal inheritance.

But we have to choose to live by His values that offend our mind;
offend our logic; offend our reasoning; offend our flesh.
Choosing to believe that He knows best.
Choosing to follow the example set by Jesus

## Temporal or eternal

In Heb 12:16  The Message Bible says

*Watch out for the Esau syndrome*

*trading away God's lifelong gift*

*in order to satisfy a short term appetite.*

How often do we get caught out by the things of the "now"?

And in doing so, we compromise what we really believe,

and have to live with the consequences of poor choices

made on impulse

but lived with for ever.

## Hearing God

Do you ever feel that you have problems in hearing God speak to you?

May I suggest that as in the natural so in the spiritual!

When wax blocks our ears, hearing is dulled.
Action needs to be taken to clear the blockage
so ..... we get your ears syringed.

In a similar way, our spiritual ears can become blocked
and hearing God becomes dulled or cut off.

If this is the case then you need to consider -

What could be blocking my spiritual ears?
Could it be a wrong attitude; a sin; an area of unforgiveness;
a preoccupation with things of the world,
including hobbies; work-life; home-life; friends?

Be radical and identify the blockage.
Be radical and clear the blockage.

Restore the communication lines with God
and walk in faith in the things that He sets before you.

## On-going prayer

1 Thess 5:17 encourages us to pray continually

or pray without ceasing.

This means that we "live" a life of prayer throughout the day

and not just "have" times set aside for prayer

although that would be "a part" of the living.

1 Peter 1 in the The Message Bible says

*Life is a journey you must travel with a deep consciousness of God*

and we need to cultivate a constant awareness of God.

We need a constant communication with God

throughout the routine of our lives,

rather than "God-slots" which become more and more

infrequent as life gets busier.

We need to be knowing a constant connection with

and a constant communication with God.

Then we will more easily "keep in step with the Spirit"

as it says in Gal 5:25

and will more easily live life and view life

from God's perspective

rather than from a worldly perspective.

## Living by the rule book

Living by rules and regulations or
giving rules and regulations to others for living the Christian life
can lead to a false sense of security.
Why?
Because we don't have to listen to the Holy Spirit
but just keep the rules and it seems OK!
Have a quiet time each morning; pay my tithe
go to church Sunday morning and cell group in the week
and always be kind to my neighbour
seems to tick all the right boxes!

But God doesn't want the boxes ticked.
God wants relationship, He has plans that we know nothing of
and He wants us to go to Him regularly,
to hear from Him where to go next;
how to handle this situation;
how to deal with that difficult relationship.
He is not predictable in what He does or how He does it.
One person is healed by a word; another has spit on his eyes;
another needs two touches; another is healed at a distance.

And God's ways are still as varied today
because He wants us to keep talking to Him,
to keep referring to Him,
to do things His way not our way.
So ... build the relationship
and live from fresh manna every day.
Not the stale bread of yesterday; last week or last month.
God's manna is fresh every day if we will collect it.

## When you're in the dark

Isa 50:10 -11
*Let him who walks in the dark, who has no light,*
*trust in the name of the Lord and rely on his God.*
*But now, all you who light fires*
*and provide yourselves with flaming torches,*
*go, walk in the light of your fires and*
*of the torches you have set ablaze.*
*This is what you shall receive from my hand:*
*You will lie down in torment.*

This verse says to me that when things seem dark
and the way ahead is not obvious
we have two choices

Either we can stay close to God and trust Him for He is the Way.
He knows the Way even in the dark for He is Light
and He doesn't dwell in darkness.
In His time things will become clear for us if we stay close.

Or we can light our own fires or torches
i.e. make our own provision,
find our own way out with logic; rational thinking or self effort.
But ...... this doesn't bring God's blessing on us,
rather, He says it will leave us in torment.

So next time you feel you're in the dark in a situation
or confused or unknowing about which direction to take,
don't forget - you have a choice.
You can take things into your own hands and mess it up.
Or you can take His hand
and walk in trust and confidence in Him

## The Whistling God

Hey there

Did you know ........

God whistles .......

He sings.........

and He laughs .........

how cool is that?

Check it out in Isaiah 5:26 and 7:18; Psalms 2:4 and

Zephaniah 3:17.

He's not just some awesome Being with no character and no

personality.

He's real and exciting so get to know the fun side of Him.

The side that causes donkeys to talk to their masters!

That causes big fish to come and save a drowning man!

That causes a fish to pop its head out of the water

with the tax money in its mouth!

Read on to catch one of the fun things God did in my life

## The Bill and the Cat !!

We had a bill, a big bill at that.
We had no money in the bank, and that was that.
But we had a leaflet through the door.
from neighbours we'd not seen before.
It said - We've lost our cat since yesterday
and there's a reward for those who say
"We've found your cat" and that was that.
Two days later and a few hours more
I found that cat outside our door
hidden behind the garden shed
that was where it had made its bed.
I called the neighbours on the phone,
they quickly came and took it home.
I'd found the cat and that was that.
A few days passed and time went by,
then on the doorstep I did spy
a bunch of flowers and a letter
and this is where all things got better.
The reward was given - a £500 cheque.
The bill unpaid I need to check -  £500 exactly that
and so it was paid by finding a cat!

Isn't God amazing, cool and exciting in the way He chooses to do things!
But it's no good running round looking for lost cats to pay your unpaid bills. He really is a God of surprises and a God of variety. He won't do the same thing next time. If He became too predictable we would not need to keep in touch with Him and it's relationship and fellowship He wants more than anything so He wants us to always be in that place where we have to ask Him what He is going to do next or how He is going to outwork the current situation for us.
Stay tuned in to Him and have expectation for surprises from God in your own situations

## His-story or my-story

History  =  His - story
My story  =  mystery

So whose story are you living – His-story or my-story?
Ask yourself the question.
Let it change your perspective on life as you get the right
balance.
It's His-story and it's like He's writing the book.
As a character in His-story
sometimes you come to the forefront in a certain storyline
but at other times you are only on the fringe,
or faded into the background but it's all about His storyline.
He has a purpose going from eternity to eternity,
and that is what we are part of.
That is what we were created for.
To be a part of His - story and outwork the part He has written
for us.
As He turns over the page to show the script for each new day
(Psalm 139:16)
Do we read what is there as He reveals it to us
and live the part He has written for us?
Or do we come with our red pen and write in our own plans
our own agendas; our own programmes?
Living a bit of His and a bit of our own, seeing it as my life,
an entity on its own to my way of thinking.
Or do we recognise our integral part in His eternal purpose?

## His strength

Are you tired, weary, worn out and stressed?
Maybe you are running with your own programme and your own
agenda as well as His and, hey, that's too much !!
He gives us strength to do those things He requires us to do.
Sufficient and enough to see things through.
But when we move to our agenda, well then .....
we're on our own with self effort and not enough strength.
It even has significance for our mind.
Think about those things He wants you to think about.
Whatsoever is good, honourable and right as in Philippians 4
and you're OK.
But ..... start thinking or worrying about other things
and we move into our own agenda again.
An agenda of worrying and anxious thoughts
and we should have given those concerns to Him,
trusted Him to work things out.
Trusted - not hoped.
So consider the situation, if it all seems too much
With not enough time or energy, ask yourself the question -
What am I carrying or seeking to do that is my own programme
or agenda?
Choose to prune your lifestyle
until it only runs with His purposes.
Then you will know peace in your heart
and stillness in your soul.
Remind yourself regularly to......
*Be still ...... and know that I am God* Psalm 46:10
He is God and He can do all things better than us.
Don't interfere in what He is trying to do.
He is more than capable!
So bow out gracefully and have a rest.

## Whose yoke are you carrying?

Good question?
So whose yoke <u>are</u> you carrying?
If everything seems a burden; a labour; a pressure
and too much stress
whose yoke are you carrying?
Jesus says in Matthew 11
*My yoke is easy and my burden is light*!
Does that sound like your experience?
If it does then stick with it
and continue to live in victory over the enemy.
But if it doesn't consider two possibilities.
Either you are sharing the yoke with Jesus but there is something
amiss in your attitude
or
you're carrying <u>your</u> yoke not His.
Running with your own programme and agendas.
Ones that are put on you by yourself, or others,
but not by Him.
Works done outside of His purposes weigh us down,
put us under pressure and bring no eternal rewards.
As it says in 1 Cor 3 - works done from our own agenda
or self effort will be burnt up like hay or straw at the end.
Works done under His yoke will be rewarded with gold and silver.
Don't put yourself under pressure with things that will go
unrewarded.
Carry the yoke with Him.
Outwork His plans and His agenda
and know peace in your spirit
stillness in your soul
and eternal rewards being added to your kingdom inheritance.

## Kingdom values or the world's values?

The world's values influence us every day from a very young age, without us even being aware of it. They so naturally become a part of us that if we want to live by kingdom values we have to make a conscious choice to do so until they are worked into the very fabric of our being.

Living by kingdom values always involves a sacrifice of self for the sake of others and is the outworking of taking up our cross.

We so easily say "Yes" to them in principle and then don't follow through in practice because it hurts the flesh.

We seek to justify ourselves and say "but this is different".

But it's not. It's just our flesh squirming!

For example, we lend something out and don't get it back or it comes back trashed but kingdom values says - it's OK!

We are offended or hurt by someone else's actions or words against us and we want to seek revenge or satisfaction.

But kingdom values offers unconditional forgiveness!

We suffer an injustice and would seek to have it put right.

Kingdom values takes it with good grace and lets it go!

And where do I get all these challenging values from?

Matthew 5 and Luke 6 "The Sermon on the Mount"

Did Jesus say it just to tickle our ears or did He mean us to live that way just as He did?

Will we choose to walk the lowly path of injustice and serving others sacrificially, believing that it is the better way from an eternal perspective, or when it raises its head in our daily situation will we sow into the ways of the world and reap the harvest it brings?

Gal 6:8 *Those who sow to please the Spirit will reap eternal life.* I think that's the harvest I prefer to have.

Invest into your eternal inheritance and know that the treasure that is building up there is free from economic downturns!

## Overcoming the spirit of the age

How can we be involved in spiritual warfare and how can we each be involved in overcoming the enemy on a daily basis ? Simply by living from the opposite spirit and by living from the values of the kingdom and not the values of the world.
Meaning?
Defeat the spirit of materialism by not having a materialistic spirit yourself or being content with what you have and not always striving for more things or always wanting the newest or latest gadgets.

Defeat the spirit that breaks down families by building a stable and strong family yourself and fighting for your marriage when it seems under pressure rather than letting it go

Defeat the spirit of stress and pressure by refusing to live life at a frantic pace. Keeping your inner being in a place of stillness and rest by choice. Stepping back when we feel the tension mounting until we have found that place of peace within oourself

Defeat the spirit of pride by seeking the good of others in preference to self. – see Phil 2:3

Defeat the spirit of revenge by being ready to forgive in all situations. It's never easy;  it always hurts; and it's a choice. A choice we need to make for our own peace of mind and for our freedom

So choose to crush the enemy by manifesting the opposite spirit and begin to see a change in the atmosphere around you.

<u>Where are you exploring?</u>

Ephesians 3 tells that God's love is too vast to comprehend
with our minds
but how much can we explore of it with our spirits?

And if His love is vast, then how vast is His joy?
And how vast is His peace?
And how vast is every other aspect of His nature?

If you are looking for a challenge or looking for an adventure
what better place to start than exploring God and His character
and your lifetime won't be long enough to complete it!

You'll never get bored
and you'll never stop being surprised by the unexpected.

But how many of us choose
to explore the Christian faith rather than God, Himself?
Explore His book rather than explore the writer of the book?

He wrote the book to reveal Himself to us
not to give us a study guide
.

Exploring the book or Christianity for its own sake gives us
knowledge but exploring God and getting to know more of Him
will bring life and power that will impact us and the overflow will
impact those around us.

## His mystery

An ear to hear, an eye to see

Those things that don't make sense to me

For from His heart

He will impart

The hidden things  -  the mystery.

## Are you a stranger?

So are you a stranger?

Psalm 119:19 in The Message Bible says

*I'm a stranger in these parts give me clear directions*

Yes! I say to that, I'm a stranger

and I want to stay a stranger

I'm going forward with God

and I am striking new ground all the time.

I haven't been here before,

I don't know the pathway ahead because I'm walking in the

things that the Father has planned for me

and it's an unknown journey.

Unexpected, unknown, Your ways not mine.

But You Jesus are the Way - You ...are .....the ....Way.

And You will take me where you will if I am available to You.

I can opt out and make my own plans, map my own pathway

but do I have confidence in myself,

or is my confidence really in You

and only in You

## Confidence in Jesus

Jeremiah 17 says

*Blessed is the man who trusts in the LORD,*

*whose confidence is in Him.*

*He will be like a tree planted by the water*

*that sends out its roots by the stream.*

*It does not fear when heat comes;*

*its leaves are always green.*

*It has no worries in a year of drought*

*and never fails to bear fruit.*

If my confidence is in You, Lord then I have hope.

But if it is in myself, what hope is there?

I want my confidence to be in You, Lord

so that .......

I don't fear the circumstances that come upon me.

I have no worries because I'm trusting in You

and so....

no matter what ......

I am always bearing fruit of the kingdom.

Keep me as a stranger, Lord

ever exploring new things with You

and stay close, always showing me the next step.

Stay close so that I am hearing what You would speak to me

## Whose expectations are you living up to?

Or whose expectations are you trying to live up to?
If you try and live up to your own expectations you can go awry
in one of two ways. Either you will be too hard on yourself and
bring yourself under condemnation because you are not
maintaining the standards you expect of yourself. Or you will be
too lenient and tolerate things within yourself that you wouldn't
tolerate in others and self-deception creeps in.
If you try and live up to other people's expectations, as you
perceive them, then again you will quite easily come under
condemnation as people move more easily in judgement than
grace. And other people's expectations will be a changeable
yardstick as those people who like you will tolerate and overlook
those things that other's with a lower opinion of you will criticise.
If you want truth wrapped in grace as to how well you're doing,
then it's God's standards and expectations you should be living
up to. If God shows us our faults it is because He wants to take us
to a better place within ourselves; to make us more like Christ.
And He doesn't point the finger and then walk away leaving us
crushed or without hope. No, He exposes the truth of what we
are and then takes our hand, if we are willing to take His, and
walks us through the process, every step wrapped in grace and
love.

But don't forget Colossians 1:22 where it tells us that we stand in
God's presence without a single fault because of the work Jesus
did on the cross. He doesn't focus on our faults. He knows we
need shaping. He focuses on the work of Christ and receives us
into His presence without seeing a single fault. But when we are
in His workshop, like a carpenter He chisels and shapes us by the
people and the situations around us to bring out those hidden
depths of beauty that only He can bring to the surface.

## Exploring other languages

Languages..... words ........pictures

Don't limit yourselves to what you know

but get out there and smell the colour nine!

God isn't limited to the spoken language

Psalm 19 tells us that the stars praise Him and sing to Him ....

without words.

That the mountains sing together for joy ..... without words.

Explore the language of music.

Instead of verbalising your prayers ... express them with music.

God understands the language of music.

Explore the language of pictures.

Instead of verbalising your prayers ..... express them with

pictures.

God understands the language of pictures.

He is creative and wants to draw out the creative in us.

Be released into new areas.

Be refreshed by the creative within you.

Step out in faith and see where God will take you.

## Let God Fight the Battles

Yes, let God "fight the battles" or "do the business" when other people are troubling you, causing you offence or being unfair or unjust - Why?

Because He does it so much better than us and without so many casualties.

If we try and deal with things ourselves we so often find bad attitudes surfacing and also we don't know a person's history or where they are coming from;

what they are dealing with from the past that makes them act as they do and all manner of other things –

but God does !!

He knows just how to handle it for the best of everyone concerned.

All He wants us to do is to spend more time with Him, just enjoying being in His presence, so that *He can take great delight in us, He can quiet us with His love and He can rejoice over us with singing*! As it says in Zeph 3:14

Are you willing to trust Him with your issues or will you continue to do it yourself.

The choice as ever is yours to make - every time!

## Secret Smiles

Yes, that's right, secret smiles.

Not as weird as "Can you smell the colour nine?" but certainly going that way. But if we want to touch the deeper things of God we have to go beyond the rational and the reasonable because God is much bigger than our mindsets and we have to be willing to break out and break free!

After the previous thought of letting God do the fighting for you let's consider the concept of secret smiles because, for me, it's the antidote to not hitting back or picking yourself up when others have hit out at you (metaphorically).

When we hold our breath, or bite our tongue or feel overlooked or snubbed by others rather than speak out, or get offended or hurt, no-one else sees or knows what self-control we have had in holding back.  Except God knows. And so it does one good at that point of dying to self to look up and have a secret smile with God, and He will smile on you as He sees and approves of your unseen actions.

So go ahead and try it and grow in God with helpful tools and strategies!

### God will meet you anywhere

Let me share the beauty of my Sunday mornings with you.
They are an oasis of peace; reflection; stillness and quiet
in the busyness of an ordinary week.
A time to fellowship with God and sit with Him.
A time when jewels are dug out from the depths of His being.
Revelation is received.
A deep long drink is taken from the river of life
and there is feasting from His table
The fellowship is rich; vibrant and satisfying.
It fills me with rich things that I can pour into the lives of others
throughout the week.
Precious times which I hate to give up unless it is really necessary
However these times of oasis are usually found in a quiet room
with my bibles and journal around, alone with God.
And yet ...... today......
as I took an extra half hour in bed, needing physical rest and
refreshment,
God met with me even there.
As I mused and meditated on the things He has been showing me
I felt the spirit stirring within me.
I felt as if I was surrounded by a golden glow.
As if His glory was resting upon me.
Even before I had gone to my chosen place of fellowship
He had come to meet with me, just where I was.
And my heart was touched by my ever-loving Father
He is awesome and I love Him

## Omnipresent

Father, You are fully immersed
throughout our life and throughout our history
throughout our present and also our future.
You are already there waiting for us,
yet ever present at the same time.
Present in all things.
Permeating all things.
Touching all things.
The essence of all things.

You are all this and more for those with eyes to see it,
to see beyond the natural, beyond the mundane.
For those who look deeper and look beyond
and see the spiritual perspective
the eternal treasure in all things

Where are you looking?
What are you seeing?

# Church in the 21st Century- Part 1

My understanding of church began to evolve in a new way when God dropped into my spirit the phrase "this isn't what church is all about"

"This isn't what church is all about", that's what dropped into my spirit and it birthed something new and fresh within me. I knew from the start that it wasn't going to be a re-shaping of church as we knew it, much the same as before with a new lick of paint. No, this wouldn't be contained within the style and format of church as we were living it, because it was a fresh expression from God's directive. As I stepped into a new place with God made myself available for anything He wanted to show me it felt much like Abraham, packing up and moving on but destination unknown. A short time later I was listening to a tape when the speaker began talking about God wanting people who were willing to step out into something new and build church like it had never been built before.

Building with no forward planning or blueprint of how it would be but willing to trust God and build week by week as He directed.

Coincidence or God-incidence?

It's pretty obvious that God was confirming the way.

And not longer after, I read a prophecy that Smith Wigglesworth had before he died in 1947.

This prophecy said that there were going to be 3 significant moves of God over the next years. Firstly there would be a fresh outpouring of the Holy Spirit across the denominations, then there would be a season of house churches, and when that season began to wane there would be a fresh wave of God, the like of which had never been seen before.

Again this encouraged me to believe that I was following the voice of God.

And so the journey began .......... expectation and anticipation of being caught up in the "now" word of God.

## Church in the 21st Century - Part 2

I sensed there was a whole new feel to this idea of church.

What we knew of church had been experienced within a

changing but fundamentally similar structure for about 2,000

years so it seemed like the only way.

We find it hard to even consider anything else because it

unsettles us and leaves us feeling insecure.

But much of church life was shaped by Constantine when he

decided that as persecution hadn't extinguished the church

then ………….

"if you can't beat 'em, let's join 'em."

And church developed within that mindset

by people seeking a system that would work,

but not seeking God.

I experienced the reality of church being a lifestyle

not a service;

being your whole character

not your Sunday morning smile.

Being your daily bread

not your Sunday morning picnic.


Jesus wants us to live kingdom life as we walk with Him.

And as we seek to live kingdom,

what we call church will become manifest in the way He wants it

to without us necessarily realising it.

And in the new season we have only touched the hem of His

garment so far.

Job 26:14 says *These are but the outer fringe of his works; how*

*faint the whisper we hear of him!*

*Who then can understand the thunder of his power?*

Although it is talking about the wonders of creation

the truth holds good.

If we have only touched the outer fringes

of His workings within this new season,

and only heard a faint whisper of what He would say about it,

how much more is in His heart?

And

can we contain or comprehend the thunder of His power?

Will we choose to walk in faith

and follow his voice when He calls us?

Or do we get unsettled

and want to hold onto what we understand and know,

even if it is limiting our spiritual growth?

## Church in the 21st Century - Part 3

I believe God wants a people who expect the unexpected;
who see wine where others only see water;
who see provision for 5,000 where others see only enough for
one.
A people who know the water of life,
where others only know the water from the well.
A people who hear God.
A people who see God in the ordinary things of life.

Like Elijah who heard the sound of heavy rain and believed God
for the rain that would end the drought.
He sent his servant, 7 times,
to look for that cloud that would bring the rain.
Not until the 7th time did the servant see a cloud just the size of
a man's fist
but Elijah kept sending him because he had heard the sound in
his spirit and he believed God.

Or like Elisha who had eyes to see God's power.
When he was surrounded by a great army he had no fear
because greater than that
he saw God's army camped around them.
He prayed that the eyes of his servant would be opened to see
the same thing so that he would move out of fear and into faith.
See God's unexpected and believe for it to happen.

## Church in the 21st Century - Part 4

We need to be people that have ears that hear the sounds of
God and believe.
Who see things from God
and hold onto them until they come into being.
We need to be a people who expect the unexpected
because God is going to do new and powerful things in our time.
Don't be like the Jewish leaders who had Jesus living amongst
them and yet they never knew Him.
They continued with their temple worship
not knowing that the One that they worshipped was walking
outside.
They believed in their heads for they were taught it regularly
but they didn't recognise it with their hearts.
Don't be so rigid in your thinking
and so fixed in what you believe in your minds
that you miss what God is doing in these time and these places.
Pray for the spirit of revelation so that the eyes of your heart
may be enlightened
to see and to be involved in all that God is doing,
today and in the future.
Be a people who expect the unexpected!
For He is a God, consistent in who He is but unpredictable in
what He will do

## Church in the 21st Century - Part 5

Church is not built on one vision that all members are supposed
to "buy into" but on each person having their own vision and the
sum total of all those visions making the bigger picture for the
vision of the group.
This allows each person to hear from God for themselves;
to receive their own vision and direction based on their own
giftings and anointing; and so be motivated to outwork it.
Each person free to support a vision or project that witnesses
with their spirit not co-erced or pressured into working in areas
that they are not anointed for.
As it says in The Message Bible  Matt 11:27
*Are you tired? Worn out? Burned out on religion?*
*Come to Me. Get away with Me and you'll recover your life.*
*I'll show you how to take a real rest.*
*Walk with Me and work with Me – watch how I do it.*
*Learn the unforced rhythms of grace.*
*I won't lay anything heavy or ill-fitting on you.*
*Keep company with me and you'll learn to live freely and lightly.*
Walking with God is supposed to be in company with Him,
sharing a yoke that isn't heavy or ill-fitting as we keep in step
with the Spirit -  see Gal 5:25

Hear God for your life
and be released into walking in His plans
not someone else's programme

## God's love for me

Your heart O lord is full of love.

Full of love for me.

It's full of love for everyone,

there's plenty and enough,

but when I come to see You Lord,

it's full of love for me.

You listen fully to all I say,

take hold of every word.

You care for how I feel or think

and all Your time's for me.

Wholly focussed, finely tuned,

the fellowship is sweet.

And as Your love pours forth for me

I'm sitting at Your feet.

Receiving life, receiving love,

choosing the better part.

For You feed my soul and build me up

as I offer You my heart

## God's Training Schools

The Training Schools of God
are not the places of excellence,
like schools of learning in the world.
Not your Oxford, or your Cambridge,
or your Harvard from abroad.
With their prestige and their honour,
and the giddy lifestyles of excess.
N0 - the Training Schools of God
are empty pits and whales bellies;
desert experiences and dark caves.
Stripped of all the trappings,
all the comforts we enjoy.
Pared down to raw essentials,
or even less for some I know.
With the winds of injustice blowing fiercely in your face,
showers of doubt and misgivings,
boulders of unfairness on which we stub our to.
But with the lack of props and crutches
and the artificial supports we put in place,
God has us where He wants us
leaning only into Him.
Drawing close and listening
to the teacher of our souls.
Hearing the voice that whispers
the ways of life and truth.
Knowing the hand that sculpts us
and shapes us as we stay
close to the loving Shepherd
who so recently walked this way.

## God's Wisdom

1 Cor 2 says in The Message Bible
*God's wisdom is something mysterious
that goes deep into the interior of His purposes and
the Spirit, not content to flit around on the surface,
dives into the depths of God,
and brings out what God planned all along*

Don't you just want to touch the mysteries of God's wisdom?
To have an insight into the interior of His purposes? - Yes!
And don't you just want to know what the Spirit brings forth
when He dives into the depths of God and brings out those things
that God has planned all along? Especially the things He has
planned for your life? - Yes!
Then get in touch with Isaiah 50:4 where it says
*The Sovereign LORD has given me an instructed tongue,
to know the word that sustains the weary.
He wakens me morning by morning,
wakens my ear to listen like one being taught.*
Develop an ear that knows how to hear the Spirit of God each
morning and throughout the day. Pick up on what the Spirit is
searching out from the heart of God and so have the words of
life; truth and encouragement firstly for yourself and then for
others.
Be someone who lives from wisdom, understanding and
knowledge from the heart of God, not from the values and ways
of the world that only lead to death

# The Bigger Picture

Have you noticed how some of us so easily become focussed on our own life as if it is the only thing that exists in the universe? Asking ourselves such questions as – am I doing enough for God? Is what I am doing valid? Am I becoming what God wants me to become? etc However, I've been considering how it's not about me and my life but it's about God and His purposes, which are eternal. His plans took shape before I was ever dreamed about and His same consistent plan will run for a good while longer beyond me. We need to be willing to walk in the unknown in many ways.

We need to chill out more and rest in Him, live by faith; exist by faith and pursue relationship with God and everything else will make sense in His way.

It's not for me to see, or to know, or to be satisfied with how it's developing. It's God's plot; God's purposes; God's plan and He knows where it is going. He just wants us to be on board and go where it goes. To respond to the opportunities that He brings our way. To look to see Him and find Him in all things and be diligent and persevere in Him.

A craftsman works and labours; shapes and moulds and on-lookers scratch their heads thinking – "What is he hoping to do? Nothing seems to be taking shape." Then, all of a sudden, towards the end, it all makes sense and we can see what he had been seeing right from the start

In the same way, God is working at something and He can see it, even now, but its definition and shape is not clear to us and we need to live with that.

The disciples didn't know what they were getting into when they followed Jesus. In their day many people gathered round and followed someone who could teach or had charisma and the disciples followed Jesus as they recognised there was something about Him but they didn't know what. I don't know whether they ever realised how radical their lifetime had been and how they would be known and remembered for many generations but they just lived what they needed to live

In a similar way Ruth just lived out her daily existence, making her decisions as she went never knowing how integral she was in being part of the genealogy of Jesus. Her faithfulness and obedience led her to the place where she married Boaz and as she looked back on her life as an old woman it would all have looked so ordinary. And that's all she knew. But we know more, we know of that future destiny that she was part of and we think she's blessed. But she never knew. And what will we never know about our ordinary life?

Our lives are not individual items standing on their own. They are merely a thread in the whole of the fabric. On their own they count for nothing. Only in their right place, lost among others do they make sense and complete the picture as God plans for them to.

It has been said that much of the work God does guiding us to our destiny unfolds in our lives unnoticed until the time of its manifestation. Seemingly insignificant aspects of our lives suddenly bloom into profound realities. The natural is transformed by the supernatural leaving us forever changed

## Certain / Uncertain

James 1:17 says *Every good and perfect gift is from above, coming down from the Father of the heavenly lights, who does not change like shifting shadows.*

Heb 13:8 says *Jesus Christ is the same yesterday and today and for ever*

Psalm 90:22 says Before the mountains were born or you brought forth the earth and the world, From everlasting to everlasting you are God.

All these verses tell us of the faithfulness and consistency of God. We need to be a people who know that God is faithful and consistent in who He is but radical and unpredictable in what He does. So we need to be willing to let go of the need to control our own lives and live in the uncertainty of walking with God and not knowing what He might bring across our pathway at any point. A people who expect the unexpected and are willing to walk freely and lightly in the plans that God has for us. We need to lift ourselves out of the predictable rut of daily routine and live in quiet anticipation of the unexpected from God. Many of God's delightful gifts into our lives or divine appointments go unnoticed for the lack of spiritual eyes that are seeing them.
As in 2 Kings 6:17 when Elisha and his servant are facing an army. Elisha sees something that his servant doesn't so Elisha prayed, "O LORD, open his eyes so that he may see." Then the LORD opened the servant's eyes, and he looked and saw the hills full of horses and chariots of fire all round Elisha.
Don't be too rational and reasonable in your thinking that you miss out on the hand of God

## Set your mind on things above

We are encouraged to set our minds on things above in Col 3:2
And in 2 Cor 4:18 it says *To fix our eyes not on what is seen, but
on what is unseen. For what is seen is temporary, but what is
unseen is eternal.*

We need to believe that the eternal is as real as the physical.
Just because we can see the actual world around us we allow
that to hinder us from seeing beyond into the eternal right now.
Consider: when a baby is in the womb it is aware of nothing.
Nothing more than the enclosed space in which it is growing and
it would consider that to be it's whole world. Yet we know that
this growing baby is surrounded by, within a matter of inches, a
very real physical world which we all know of. It's noisy; alive;
vibrant; active. But try telling that to an unborn baby. It can't
begin to imagine the concept that you are talking about. In the
same way the eternal realm surrounds us and is that close to us,
just a breath away.  If we reach out in our spirit, regularly, we can
become increasingly in touch with what is going on out there.
Be willing to step out, in faith, and step into a spiritual awareness
of something more valid; more real; more effective and powerful
than all that you experience now.

## Walking with God

A daily walk with God based on Jeremiah 33:3 where God says *Call unto me and I will answer you, and tell you great and unsearchable things that you did not know."* How exciting is that? For it says in 1Cor 1:25 *For the foolishness of God is wiser than man's wisdom, and the weakness of God is stronger than man's strength.* Yes, even God's foolish thoughts are more profound than man's wisest thoughts so I want to know more of what God can tell me and teach me.

Job 26:7-14 says *He spreads out the northern skies over empty space;*
*He suspends the earth over nothing.*
*He wraps up the waters in his clouds, yet the clouds do not burst under their weight.*
*He covers the face of the full moon, spreading his clouds over it.*
*He marks out the horizon on the face of the waters for a boundary between light and darkness.*
*The pillars of the heavens quake, aghast at his rebuke.*
*By his breath the skies became fair;*
*And these are but the outer fringe of his works; how faint the whisper we hear of him!*
*Who then can understand the thunder of his power?*

He suspends the earth over nothing! How? And these are but the outer fringe of his works. So what else does He do and how can we even glimpse it ?

He wraps up the waters in his clouds, yet the clouds do not burst under their weight. Who could have thought of a water system like that? Not man, that's for sure! Man would have had some massive unwieldy monstrosity that wouldn't have worked for very long without having a breakdown in the system, and yet God thought clouds up for water storage. How awesome is that? And yet these are but the outer fringe of his works! Have you got the idea yet? I find God to be truly awesome and want to walk closer with Him to more easily hear what He wants to share.

Living from the largeness of God

Know the God you relate to. Listen to His voice
so that you can speak His life to others and encourage them,
having been first encouraged yourself.
Be strong; be confident in your God.
Let your trust and security be in Him
so that you will not be unsettled by circumstances.
Look to Him in all that you do.
Look to Him as every situation assails you and see it from His
perspective.
See it from an eternal perspective.
See it with eyes of faith.
See it in the largeness of God
and not the narrowness of your own thinking.
Not the narrowness of your own experience.
As you increasingly align your days with Him
then you will know the narrowness of your experience
and the narrowness of your thinking
enlarging and extending in the largeness of God

Jesus says in John 8 in The Message Bible
*You decide according to what you can see and touch.*
*I don't make judgements like that.*
*But even if I did, my judgement would be true because*
*I wouldn't make it out of the narrowness of my experience,*
*but in the largeness of the One who sent Me*

And later in the same chapter He says
*You're tied down to the mundane.*
*I'm in touch with what is beyond your horizons.*
*You live in terms of what you see and touch.*
*I'm living on other terms.*

## Released into our uniqueness in Him

As Jesus bought us with a price
and paid the cost with His life,
then our life is now His, redeemed and free.
And it's not just our individual sins, one-by-one
but the sin question itself is dealt with.
We are restored to that position of "before the fall."
We now choose to eat from the tree of life
and turn our backs on the tree of knowledge of good and evil.
We choose to defer to God in all things,
dependent on Him for life and truth and knowledge.
Depending on Him, but not controlled.
Released and free to live to the full potential
of what He first created.
To express and release all that He has planted in us.
To live our unique qualities of character and personality.
To live our unique expression of the gifts He has put within us.
And as we each live in the fullness of our uniqueness
so there will be a richness in the colours and vibrancy
of the tapestry of life, that is being woven even now,
and into the realms of eternity.

## Come; Sit; Learn

The Father wants a people who will
come and sit at His feet and learn from Him.

We have absorbed so much over the years that is
tradition; history or culture
that we are in danger of living from the
Tree of the Knowledge of Good and Evil.
We are in danger of living from the mind of man
and not the heart of God.
He wants us to go with open hearts and open minds
willing to have our teachings and doctrines
turned up-side down or thrown out the window
if they aren't in line with the heart of God for today.

His storehouses of wisdom, understanding and knowledge are
limitless and yet we so easily limit ourselves to the crumbs
that have been received from history and other people.

He wants us to open our eyes, open our ears, open our hearts
and quieten our spirits and to regularly seek His face
for today's truth, today's word of life.
Different for each person, individual to each person.
He wants to give us precious gems; treasures of truth
not paste jewels that we have collected from the past.

So come and sit at His feet and learn from Him.
Know your life being enriched with things of eternal value
as you feast at His table and drink from the fountain of life.

## Preconceptions

We all approach the Bible with certain preconceptions

dependent on our current thinking or doctrine.

So we read the word and squeeze it to fit our doctrine,

which isn't helpful sometimes if our doctrine is a bit askew.

In a similar way,

if we do not carry grace and mercy in our hearts

then we will interpret the Word legalistically

and to the letter of the law.

Just as the Pharisees did with the woman taken in adultery.

Whereas Jesus, who carries grace and mercy in His heart,

approached her differently.

And so ………..

How many people have been damaged over the years

by a legalistic use of the Word,

rather than wrapping it in grace and mercy

before we deliver our judgement?

Revelation or Law

When you move or act without revelation

you move into law

and it produces death.


If you move or act from revelation

it produces life.


Man gives law.

God gives revelation.

## Opportunities or Obstacles?

Opportunities or obstacles? Adventures or problems?
What do we see in our situations?
Our answer is rooted in our knowledge of the Father.
if we really knew Him then we would receive everything as an
opportunity or an adventure in Him.
If I can only see everything as it relates to the here and now
then it is rooted in self-awareness.
We so easily think - my life has to be worthwhile either in God's
purposes
or in achieving my own goals
but that is looking from a wrong perspective.
We feel driven to show that "my life is worthwhile."
In God's economy that can look very different to what the world
or we ourselves want to see.
It's God's life - we're in His hands.
He wants to outwork His purposes
and we tangle things up when we introduce our own agenda.
Perpetual motion isn't necessary.
Settle into His plans.
Busy in His plans doesn't bring pressure.
He bears the weight of the yoke.
He is ultimately responsible.
Rest in His purposes - busy but at rest.
Inner peace - inner stillness.
Don't seek to prove something that doesn't have to be proved.
It's not about joining up - it's about living kingdom life
and living in relationship with God and with others.
It's about being conformed into His likeness through our daily
situations.
Not self-seeking or demanding our rights or fair treatment
but - reflecting His nature and His character of grace, humility
meekness and kindness.

## Truth or tradition

Have you seriously considered

whether some of the things that you believe

are based on tradition and the teachings of man

rather than truth as revealed from the heart of God?

Have you held things against the truth of scripture to see how

valid they are?

We don't want to be bound by the thoughts of man

but released into the freedom of truth from God.

Let us live by the revealed truth from the heart of God

not the traditions, philosophies or doctrines from the mind of

man

## Pioneers for something new

God is doing something new at this time.

It's a new season for a new age.

No longer church system but Kingdom

and as we go out and explore this new age

we are like the spies sent to the Promised Land.

Some are seeing something good in what God is revealing to
them,

willing to walk a lonely pathway as they forge ahead,

like Joshua and Caleb of old.

But others are easily frustrated and lacking vision

and without numbers joining with them

they easily give up and go back to the old.

Like the 10 other spies they don't have eyes of faith,

but are looking for tangible results before they go there.

They see the negative aspects more than the blessings God is
giving in that place.

If you're a pioneer – hold fast to what you have seen in the spirit

and in God's time it will come to pass.

He wants a people who bring to earth

His purposes which are formed in heaven.

## Receiving the Bread of Life

When we receive truth or manna from God

we sometimes want to keep hold of it

fully understand it

and work through it with our mind.

We are concerned that within a week we may have forgotten it

because of other things that God has been showing us.

But ...... consider what happens with natural food.

We don't need to understand the workings of the digestive

system, nutrition values or anything else.

So long as we take in the food and absorb it

it does its work in a natural way without us fully understanding,

without us seeking to be involved in the application.

In a similar way - as we receive truth or manna from God,

If we receive it, believe it and by faith absorb it as life

then it will do its work within us.

Feeding our spirit and nurturing us

in a way we won't necessarily understand or be a part of

but then that's the bigness of God!!!

## Learn from Me

I feel the word God has given me for this season is

"Come and sit at my feet and learn from Me"

How exciting - as it suggests that He definitely has things
that he wants to share with me.
However - it also causes me to consider -
How much of what I know have I actually learned from Him
and how much is just passed down tradition
or man-made beliefs?
Check out some of your beliefs to the true judgement
of scripture and see if they still really hold good.
What is truly of God will stand up to scrutiny,
but some of our long-held beliefs may fall by the wayside
as not being supported by scripture
and we need to consider how we will handle those issues.

## Worship

Rom 12:1 says
*I urge you, brothers, in view of God's mercy,*
*to offer your bodies as living sacrifices, holy and pleasing to God.*
*This is your spiritual act of worship.*

So .... what is our understanding of worship?
It doesn't seem to be singing songs and worship bands
from what we read in Romans 12

If worship is honouring God and declaring that
He is worthy of honour, praise and many other things,
then I suggest that some of our attitudes and mindsets
are dishonouring to God
and therefore, the opposite of worship.

For example –
if we worry, fret or are anxious about life's issues
or the situations we find ourselves facing
then we are not trusting God in those things
and so we dishonour Him.
Our anxiety says - I cannot trust You - therefore I'm worrying
and we dishonour Him in that way.

So, conversely if we trust Him for our situations
and that is evident by our peace our inner rest and stillness
then we acknowledge He is worthy
and that is an act of worship.
So worship is a lifestyle not a group activity.
It is manifest in different ways for each of us.
So identify what would be your acts of worship
having seen what attitudes or mindsets dishonour Him
and live a life of daily worship.

# Psalm 119

Psalm 119 is a brilliant psalm when read in The Message Bible
and some of my favourite phrases from it are -

1)  *I'm a stranger in these parts - give me clear directions.*

If we are constantly going forward with God
we should always be in new places and needing His direction
and that is one of the ways He keeps us pressing into Him.

2) *My sad life's dilapidated, a falling down barn, build me up
again by Your Word.*

Yes - David's life seems rubbish to him at that point
and we can be the same sometimes.
However, he knows that it is God's Word that will build him up
again
rather some crutch like comfort food, drink, TV, sport
or whatever it is that makes you feel good.
It is only the Word of God that can do a real work in us.
The rest is just a temporary fix

3)  *Your truth never goes out of fashion.*
*It's as up-to-date as the earth when the sun comes up*

Not like the politics of the day; the fashions of the moment;
the morals of the generation or the food fads just now.
No - God's truth never goes out of fashion
and the values that were relevant for kingdom life 2,000 years
ago
still hold good for today
and will still be good for every day to come.

## Yahweh

God is a very general term - short and abrupt.

Yahweh is His name.

Yahweh means 'always'.

and He is ..... always.

Always loving, always there, always just, always steadfast

always – Yahweh.

So, more often than not, I am choosing to refer to Him

by His name - Yahweh

not short, not abrupt but easy on the tongue

soft like a breath.

The creative living breath – Yahweh

## David's Psalms

David wrote the Psalms

because ……

he knew the reality of these truths in his life.

He knew God's protection in battle.

He knew Jesus as a shepherd.

But then we just pluck them out of the scriptures

and seek to see them realised in our own life

but without the reality, history or experience behind us.

If we wrote our own Psalm ……

How would it read?

What could we give testimony to?

We can't live on David's inheritance,

we have to have our own.

So …… make it personal.

Write your own Psalm

and be encouraged by the testimony

that you carry

of the realities of God in your life.

## What are my values?

The world values riches and achievements and success.
However
Jeremiah says in chapter 9
*Don't boast about your wisdom, strength or riches*
*Rather boast that you know the Father*
*and understand Him*
*He who exercises kindness and justices*
*for the Father delights in those people*

and in a similar vein in Psalm 119 (The Message Bible)
David says -
*I delight far more in what you tell me about living*
*than in gathering a pile of riches*

What do I boast in and what do I delight in?
The things that this world values?
Or the things of eternal value?

## Let there be light

Psalm 119:130 says
*Break open Your Word  -  Let the light shine out.*
Unless God breaks open His word to us it is no more than words
on paper.
However, when He breaks it open it imparts truth, life and power
into our lives and spirits.
But when we look for the light to shine out from the broken word
we need to remember our physics lessons where we learnt that a
beam of white light when it passes through a glass prism breaks
open into a rainbow of different colours.
When we look for the light to shine out as God breaks His word
open to us we can limit ourselves to one beam of white light and
have a measure of impartation or we can have expectation, by
faith, for it to break open in a vast array of colour and receive the
fullness of what God was wanting to give us.
Believe - bigger than your understanding - bigger than before.
Believe the awesome God for bigger things.
It says in Ephesians 3:20
*By His mighty power at work within us*
*God is able to accomplish infinitely more*
*than we would ever dare to ask or hope*!
Dare to believe God for impartation and revelation that goes
beyond the norm.
Anyone can do normal, but with God we can do and have the
impossible.
Can you smell the colour nine?
Yes - I really said it - can you smell the colour nine?
Even if your mind says whhhaaattt? let your spirit shout YES and
let something creative stir within you.
Get out there and explore God

## Losing our peace

What is it that robs us of our peace?
Cares, anxieties, worries and concerns.
Call them what you like they all add up to the same thing.
A troubled mind!
But Jeremiah 17 talks about the man who trusts in the LORD,
whose confidence is in God.
It says he will be like a tree planted by the water
that sends out its roots by the stream.
It does not fear when heat comes;
its leaves are always green.
It has no worries in a year of drought
and never fails to bear fruit.

It is saying – the one who trusts God will always be at peace no
matter what his circumstances for he chooses to give His worries
to God to work out.
And this is in response to 1 Peter 5:7 which says that
we should give Him our anxiety.
Why? Because He cares for us.

Phil 4 says that His peace will actually guard
our heart and mind if we offload our concerns to him.

and Matt 6:33 encourages us to use our minds
for seeking the matters of the kingdom
while God deals with our concerns and our needs for each day.

## Peace in our inner being

Peace is a tool giving strength to ourselves
and in defeating the enemy.
Satan constantly tries to unsettle us and rob us of our peace

But Psalm 34:14 says *Seek peace and pursue it.*

We have to take action in keeping our peace.

Don't let satan rob you of your peace,
but fight for it, seek it, and pursue it

The key to being in peace is found in Romans 8:6
*The mind controlled by the Spirit is life and peace*

Are we willing to release the control of our mind and allow God
to lead us, guide us and give us the opportunity to follow what
He shows to be best?
Or does our old nature cling onto control?

Release the mind to the control of the Spirit
and give yourself the opportunity to live freely and lightly.

# We're all unique – Embrace your Uniqueness

An elderly Chinese woman had two large pots, each hung on the ends of a pole which she carried across her neck. One of the pots had a crack in it while the other pot was perfect and always delivered a full portion of water. At the end of the long walk from the stream to the house, the cracked pot arrived only half full. For a full two years this went on daily, with the woman bringing home only one and a half pots of water.

Of course, the perfect pot was proud of its wonderful accomplishments. But the poor cracked pot was ashamed of its own imperfection, and miserable that it could only do half of what it had been made to do.

After 2 years of what it perceived to be bitter failure, it spoke to the woman one day by the stream. "I am ashamed of myself, because this crack in my side causes water to leak out all the way back to your house."

The old woman smiled, "Did you notice that there are flowers on your side of the path, but not on the other pot's side?" "That's because I have always known about your flaw, so I planted flower seeds on your side of the path, and every day while we walk back, you water them. For two years I have been able to pick these beautiful flowers to decorate the table. Without you being just the way you are, there would not be this beauty to grace the house."

Each of us has our own unique flaw.
But it's the cracks and flaws we each have that make our lives together so very interesting and rewarding.

You've just got to take each person for what they are and look for the good in them.

So, to all of my crackpot friends, have a great day and remember to smell the flowers on your side of the path!

## The Father's Heart

I believe the Father is looking for people who have heard His
voice and are willing to walk with Him.
Who have heard His heart for this new season and are willing to
follow His voice into the unknown just walking step-by-step with
Him.
With no manifest evidence to validate or justify their walk
but willing to go, secure only in what He has said.
People who live from His daily revelation not from the crumbs of
others or the traditions of the fathers.
For He gives fresh manna daily, which is
vibrant, life-giving, full of truth and wisdom for today.
He is looking for people who are willing to be strangers
constantly walking in new areas with Him.
Dancing to the tune of His revelation,
not the plans or programmes of men.
People who know themselves to be part of a bigger picture.
One character in His story ...
not the main character in their own story.
Living out of relationship, free from the bondage of law or
religion..
Living free from restriction, in a spacious place,
feasting at the Father's table,
drinking from the fountain of life.
Knowing the abundant life, found in His presence.
Reflecting the Father's glory and His character.
People who have hearts to hear His mysteries and not to discard
them through rationality.
Who live in the largeness of God not in the narrowness of their
own experience or thinking.
Who receive, not by studying with the mind, but by impartation.
from the heart of God
Unlocking the hidden mysteries of God by the breath of the Spirit
in their lives

## Rest in what I am doing

God heart is for us to rest in what He is doing,
not to be busy with what we want to do.

It's too easy to have our own plans for the day,
the next week and the next month.
And it takes time to listen to God
and to hear what He is saying

But ... if we want to bear fruit for the kingdom
If we want to invest into our eternal inheritance

We need to ...
Rest in what He is doing
Not in what we want to do

Then we will be living in the freedom and rest that Jesus talks
about in Matthew 11:28 (The Message Bible)

*Are you tired? Worn out? Burned out on religion? Come to me.*
*Get away with me and you'll recover your life. I'll show you how*
*to take a real rest. Walk with me and work with me—watch how I*
*do it. Learn the unforced rhythms of grace. I won't lay anything*
*heavy or ill-fitting on you. Keep company with me and you'll learn*
*to live freely and lightly.*

## How different is your life?

I was challenged by the question
"If a moral, good-living non-christian asked you
in what way was your life different to theirs, how would you
answer them?"

and this would be my answer -

Because of my relationship with the Living God
I don't live at the mercy of my circumstances,
or at the mercy of myself.
I am secure in myself and have peace and confidence in life
because I know that someone greater than I is in control.
I have hope and confidence and I know my future destiny.
I am not unsettled by what goes on in the natural world
because I know there is more going on in the spiritual world.
Because I have released my life to God and choose to come
under the lordship of Christ,
I know that I am part of an eternal plan and my life has eternal
purpose.
My values in life and my moral code for living are not changeable
and influenced by the times or the culture I live in,
but they are stable and steadfast through the centuries
because they are based on the Creator's manual.

So what would your answer be, to that same question, I wonder?

## Peace

Peace is a tool

Peace is a weapon

Peace is a victory

Peace is power

Peace is strength

Peace is an act of worship

Peace is yours - at any time

Find the pathway to peace

Know the pathway to peace

Choose to live in peace

## Keep your spiritual eyes open

We can often miss out on good things from God because they
don't come as expected.
In the time of Moses the tabernacle looked like a dull
insignificant item because outwardly it was covered with animal
skin,
and yet it was full of all sorts of earthly treasures and housed the
very presence of God.
So I am provoked to keep my eyes and ears open for unlikely
sources of seeing God's treasures and gems into my life.
Things I would normally disregard as worthless and yet in God
they carry great value.
How often do we miss a means of God's grace to us because we
reject the packaging in which it comes?
How many people do we disregard or brush aside because they
do not fit the right image for us?
Did Naaman really want to be told by a young servant girl where
he could find his healing from leprosy?
He certainly didn't want to immerse himself in the dirty
River Jordan as the prophet told him to.
He much preferred the clean rivers in his own country,
but his healing wasn't to be found where he wanted it.
It was the River Jordan or nothing.
How often do we reject what God sends our way?
How often do we reject people that God brings to us
because they don't meet our expectation?
Or we don't like the packaging?
Keep your spiritual eyes open and be ready to receive all that
comes from God.
If you only stop for what meets with your approval you may be in
danger of missing that which has true supernatural substance.

## An ear to hear

An ear to hear.

An eye to see.

The wonders of your mystery.

As You impart.

to a simple heart,

the secrets from eternity.

## Killing the Truth

In John 8:37  Jesus says to the people

*And yet some of you are trying to kill me because*

*my message does not find a place in your hearts*!

And what is the parallel in our times?

We can't literally kill Jesus but …….

He says, Himself, I AM THE TRUTH

and how many of us are guilty of trying to "kill the truth"

because it does not find a place in our hearts or in our doctrine?

Like the Pharisees we can hold so fast to our traditions,

doctrines and "constructed truth" that we won't let go

and receive God's word of truth or revelation for today.

Many of our truths and doctrines were "constructed"

to fit man's own agenda especially man's need for control.

So …. We have regular gatherings, in assigned buildings

with appointed leaders who feel safe as they keep control.

But God is speaking a word today that we need to respond to

and let go of all the traditions that hold us back

and walk in His revealed truth of today.

## Know His Way Through the Dust of Man

Often our days are unsettled or disturbed by the dust of man
which gets in our eyes; clouds our vision
and generally disturbs us for some while.

Recognise what is the dust of man in your life,
what situations cloud your mind or disturb your peace.
Then be on your guard, be alert to those things
and be proactive in attacking them for what they are.

Identify those people who kick up dust in your life
so you can have ready the shield of faith to deflect the barbs.

Don't see it as personal but as the enemy seeking to rob you
of the abundance of life that Jesus promised.
Hold fast to the truth and enjoy the spoils of war.

## Mould Each Day into the Truth of God

Mould each day into the truth of God....
What a statement is that!

As a result of its prompting I find it helpful to consider each
morning  - this is a new day - shape it; mould it.
In your mind and in your thinking
align the day with the truths from God.
Truths that declare - God is good.
He has things assigned for me today - some I am aware of
some I don't yet know - so I need an ear tuned to His voice.
This is a day to experience His abundant life,
His hand of favour upon me,
in whatever form His favour takes.
Don't try to presume what His favour means
but allow Him to show what His favour means.
Seek to experience His salvation in tricky situations,
to know His wisdom when necessary
and to live from kingdom values.

So I seek to take each day as it arrives
to mould it; warm it; soften it
and to put an impression on it - that is the mark of God.
To press His seal into it and step out
with hope and expectation.

More from Psalm 119

*You're my place of quiet retreat*
*I wait for Your word to renew me*
says David in The Message Bible

The world is ever-developing new ideas,
philosophies and programmes
to help people deal with the stress of this life.
All manner of techniques, tactics and strategies
to refresh our bodies as the stress of life takes its toll.
From yoga and pilates to massage and sauna
to name but a few.

But......... in Psalm 119,
David shows that he has found the real answer to life.
He simply says ... *You're my place of quiet retreat*
*I wait for Your word to renew me.*
Look no further; pay no money.
Learn to live as David did
and live in the experience of
My soul finds rest .... where? ....... in God alone.

## Grace

Grace feels like a welcome when you're expecting a shrug.

Grace feels like joy when you're expecting sadness.

Grace looks like hope when you're expecting despair.

Grace looks like acceptance when you expected rejection.

Grace hangs around when you feel lonely

and above all ......

grace is forgiveness when you didn't deserve any.

Thank God for His grace and His mercy.

## True Spirituality

True Spirituality isn't only expressed in places of retreat

and solitary times.

These are times for rest, refreshment and restoring

our inner being

so that .... we can go out to express our spirituality

as we face the issues of the real world

in our daily situations.

Faith -vs- Science

Science suggests Christians are gullible people
who believe ideas not based in fact or logic
and have ideas that are inconsistent with scientific
understandings.

However in a recent column in our daily paper,
a junior doctor suggests the thought that
much of science is also an article of faith
and he goes on to say

"After all, I've never seen an electron
and have no way of proving that they really exist.
We believe they exist because we're told they do.
And what can be more fantastical than the notion of atoms?
I can't even prove how some of the drugs I prescribe work!"

Interesting thoughts don't you think!

## Quality or Quantity

What is eternity - quantity or quality?

Quantity is just "for ever"

whereas quality is rich; abundant; fullness of all things.

Jesus promised quality not quantity in John 10:10


So how are you living?

Are you just living for quantity

or are you living the adventure of quality?

<u>Head or heart</u>

Receive a word in your mind

and you will have something to talk about.

Receive a word in your heart or spirit

and you will have something to live.

Where is your receiver?

Mind or Spirit?

## Where are you walking?

Do not leave me wandering

where You were yesterday, Father,

but lead me by the hand

to where You are today.

God is always moving on and unless we keep in step with Him

by the Spirit

then we will get left in yesterday's purposes;

last week's or last month's purposes.

We need to be moving on as God moves on so my heart says

Do not leave me wandering

where You were yesterday, Father,

but lead me by the hand

to where You are today.

## Keywords

Words can be keys to unlock situations

and so we have "keywords."

A keyword will unlock a situation and bring freedom.

Do you know the keyword

that will unlock the current situation you are struggling with?

The word that will bring freedom or release to the person you

are praying for?

The  word that will release the prophetic word that was spoken

over you?

Keywords can bring focus and clarity

from the clutter of many words, many thoughts, many ideas.

*So seek out the keyword and unlock those things that are closed.*

## Challenges and Problems

How do you view the challenges and problems

we face day to day ?

Do you view them from earth's limitations?

Or ........

do you see them from God's perspective

with the back-up of

Heaven's unlimited power?

You will feel weighed down if you only see ...

earth's limitations

but ......

you will have faith to overcome

when you believe

for Heaven's power.

## Position is important

As it stands - alone - a musical note has no value.

No identity, no message, no significance

nothing ......

Only when it is positioned on the music stave

does it have any meaning

and it is the position that gives it identity.

The position determines the note, the pitch, the sound.

And the position, in relation to other notes, extends and adds to

the fullness of how they sound.

Harmony..... or discord ......?

All determined by position and related or surrounding notes.

So what are the spiritual parallels for us?

Where are you positioned?

Does your position put you in a melody

or in crashing discord?

## A letter on its own

As a musical note, on its own, has no identity or value

so a letter on its own has no meaning.

Only when placed amongst others does it then say anything,

or communicate a message.

If  each person represents a letter

then does each church represent a word

built from the letters within?

And does each city speak a sentence

from the words of each church in the city?

Does each nation speak a paragraph or maybe a chapter?

And does the world speaks the whole message?

Jesus is the Word or the Message – complete.

And it takes the whole world to reflect

what He carries in Himself.

## Reference Points

What are my reference points for life and situations and

decisions?

Am I bound by rationality; common sense

the natural laws of this world?

Or

have I broken free into the spiritual dynamics?

Am I believing in the invisible,

expecting the impossible,

living from the spiritual order of things?

Am I taking steps of faith,

knowing that each step of faith

is overshadowed by the Spirit of God?

So where the way ahead may seem dark or uncertain

don't let the devil speak doubt or fear.

See it as the overshadowing of the Spirit of God,

the covering of His wings,

and take comfort from His protection and nearness

## Thoughts from a friend

Let me share a thought I received from a friend
because it expresses a lot of what I feel myself

Church is so much bigger than anything we can comprehend to
date.

The more we try to identify church the more we tie it down.

Our earthly descriptions are become lead weights

and keep it grounded.

It's so much bigger!

And as other people round the globe are considering -

There is a mighty change coming

that will radically change the way the world defines church.

And it's not a change of doctrine

but a change in basic church life.

And it will turn upside-down most of what we thought we knew.

We will need to live from revelation not information

if we are going to keep in step with what the Spirit is doing

in our times   (Gal 5:25)

## All you need

The verse I am blessed by at the moment is 2 Pet 1:3-4
*His divine power has given us everything we need*
*for life and godliness through our knowledge of Him.*

Through our knowledge of Him and relationship with Him
we have everything we need for life and godliness.
It is there for us, and freely available, if we draw Him into our
lives and abide in Him and rest in Him.
Just knowing Him and fellowshipping with Him
empowers us for everything He wants us to do.
We can fellowship with Him at any time in any place.
Even when we are in our beds and waiting to sleep
we can spend that time with Him.
There is no cost, no appointments, no need for qualifications,
just a hungry heart and a thirsty soul can feast at His table
and drink from the fountain of life.
And His table is always full, His fountain is always flowing.
No crumbs, no scraps, no shortage,  just abundance and richness.
So if you feel like a pauper, or you feel dry or weary
then go - go to the banqueting table that is provided for you
and eat to your heart's content.

## One snowflake

One snowflake on its own is

small; delicate; fragile;  unstable in its make-up.

And yet, with one snowfall the whole landscape can be changed.

A seemingly complete new world set out before us.

What are the spiritual parallels?

Each of us, individually, are important

and valuable to the complete picture.

The sum of the small individuals can have an enormous impact.

But do the conditions have to be right?

A low temperature will hold the snow in its solid state

for an indefinite period of time.

But hit that critical temperature of warm

and it's lost to another dimension – water.

What is the spiritual parallel to that?

What effect does the spiritual climate have

on the overall picture?

What effect does the spiritual climate have on you?

## What would it be like without Him?

In Colossians 1:17 it says  -

*He sustains all things by His powerful word*

*He holds all things together.*

He permeates all things.

So consider this, that oxygen is a vital part of water

even though we can't identify the oxygen as a separate item.

Yet, without the oxygen $H_2O$

would just be H, would just be hydrogen.

And hydrogen is a gas - not water,

so we would have a gas but no water.

In the same way without the presence of Jesus

what would the world and creation look like?

Interesting question to consider.

## Speak to me

Speak in ways I don't expect,
in ways that I've not known before.
An expression or manifestation of life or truth or word.
Enlarge my capacity for receiving.
Extend my expectation so that I might touch You,
I might find You
in unexpected ways and in surprising places.
Enlarge; extend and go beyond
the realms, so small, that I have known.
And let the journey take me far beyond where I've been before.
Not to follow a well-worn track,
revisiting tried and tested ways,
but making the first footsteps in virgin snow.
Making fresh footprints in the unblemished sand.
Pioneering, moving forward,
exploring and discovering
landscapes and vistas that You, O Lord,
have specially sourced for me.
Stir the anticipation, arise the expectation
and tread new ground, ride new waves
and be satisfied with nothing less.

<u>God speaks</u>

Have you considered that
God speaks in the language you know best.
Not through your ears
but through your circumstances.

Often we find ourselves struggling through our circumstances.

Just trying to get through them.

Seeking to survive them.

And we miss the real reason for them,

and don't hear the message from God

that He is trying to speak through them.

So read your circumstances with the mind of Christ

and they will lose the dull grey of the hopelesss situation

and become full technicolour in the purpose of God.

## Old truth or living Word

God's nature and being is unchanging

but we know from history that our understanding of Him

can be off-centre.

So, take a reality check and ask yourself

"Is all that I believe or think God's truth for today

or is it past it's "sell by date"?

Am I holding on to things rooted in tradition

and familiarity?

Or am I living from the living Word of God

for today?"

<u>How am I living?</u>

Am I living the Christian life
or
am I living a relationship with God?
--

Do I draw God into my life
or
do I inhabit His life?
--

Am I living from information
or
am I living from revelation?
--

There is definitely a difference
and we need to know which is true for me.

## It's my choice

We all have difficult people in our lives.

Those we struggle with for all manner of different reasons.

But how do I let them influence my life?

The choice is always mine.

I can let the situation be a trigger point

to launch me deeper into my relationship with Jesus

and be involved in the shaping of making me more like Him.

Or I can let them be a negative factor

and let them hold me back in my growth,

and let them compound my negative attitudes.


But, the choice is always mine.

I can't blame them for my bad reactions and responses.

The choice is always mine.

## Know your destiny

1 Cor 2:9 says

*No eye has seen, no ear has heard, no mind has conceived*

*what God has prepared for those who love him*

**but** *God has revealed it to us by his Spirit.*

Do you know what God has prepared for us?

I can't say I have much idea.

But it does say that He will reveal it to us by His Spirit.

Maybe I need to ask more

for Jeremiah 33:3 says

*Call unto Me and I will answer you*

*and tell you great and unsearchable things that you do not know.*

So often it isn't God who is meagre in the telling

but us who are meagre in the enquiring or searching out.

## Message in the sky

Psalm 19 says  -  *The heavens declare the glory of God;*
*the skies proclaim the work of his hands*
*Day after day they pour forth speech;*
*night after night they display knowledge*
*There is no speech or language where their voice is not heard*
*Their voice goes out into all the earth, their words to the ends of*
*the world.*

God speaks through the skies and the heavens.

Do we look for Him in unexpected places?

Does He speak to me through the skies and the heavens?

Elijah saw a message in the fist-sized cloud.

It spoke to him of coming rain.

Abraham saw a message in the stars in the sky.

It spoke to him of his heritage and descendants.

Stephen when he was stoned saw a message in the sky.

It spoke to him of a hope beyond death and

a Saviour who was waiting to receive him.

The wise men saw a message in the star.

It spoke to them of the birth of Jesus.

Noah saw a message in the rainbow.

It spoke of God's promise to mankind.

Don't limit God to past experiences.

Look for Him in unexpected places.

Hear Him where He wants to speak.

Not where you want to hear Him.

<u>Today's strength</u>

Lamentations 2:22 says
*The faithful love of the LORD never ends!*
*His mercies never cease.*
*They are new every morning.*
*Great is his faithfulness;*

God's mercy, strength and grace are new every morning,

but they are sufficient for the day alone,

not for another day.

So ..... don't drain today of today's supplies by letting them

leak away to concerns of tomorrow.

They won't touch tomorrow

but they'll drain from today.

Invest yourself fully into now

Relax into the moment

## Yokes of bondage

Don't let others put you under their yoke
which then becomes bondage.
Know your own pathway and journey.
Know your own destiny and calling from Him
and live it to your full potential.
As it says in Matt 11:28  in The Message Bible
*Walk with Him, work with Him and see how He does it*
*learn to live freely and lightly*
*learn the unforced rhythms of grace*

His yoke for you is easy.
The yoke imposed by others becomes a burden.
Don't walk someone else's pathway.
Walk your own journey and keep in step with the Spirit.

Reflections; shadows and echoes

A reflection has nothing of itself.
It is only an image of something else.


An echo has no message of its own.
It only repeats the message of another.


A shadow has no substance of itself.
it is only a pale comparison of another
and outside of the light it is lost,
it is nothing.


Be more reflective of Jesus.
Speak as an echo of His thoughts.
Nothing of self - all of Him.

## Words Unspoken

Words, from God, can be unspoken.

Not heard by the ear

or received into the mind.

Not communicated with natural language

but received into the spirit.

Received by revelation or experience

and it is the sense of it that is picked up on.

The effect is real and evident

even if not understood by the mind.

For it is spiritually understood and known

and imparts something to us in an unseen way.

## Living Free

God does not work within the confines of anything or anyone.

He will not be tied down or tied in to anything

and He wants us to live the same.

He wants us to beblown by the wind of the Spirit

with freedom, grace and mercy.

Always pushing out the boundaries of what we've known before.

Always pushing out the boundaries of what we've lived before.

Constantly exploring new territory with Him.

Ever seeking new depths in Him.

Increasing our capacity for more of Him.

## Trees of the orchard?

Let us consider that we are all a tree in God's orchard. He has planted and tended us, and we bear His fruit.

Each tree bears different fruit - we are all different species and varieties. This is something we need to bear in mind. That person we don't get on with may well be a different fruit tree completely - a pear tree whilst we are busy producing apples. This doesn't make what they do any less valid - in God's eyes, or ours!

We can only produce the fruit God gives us. And this is, also, all we have to offer. Even if we want to meet everyone's needs, we can only offer from what God has given us. If we haven't had a similar experience we may well have no fruit to offer. We need to accept that we can't be everything to all people, and just be what we are meant to be, to the fullness of our potential.

The fruit we produce is the result of what God is doing in us. We can then offer this fruit to others, to show them God and to give them food for their journey.
Being used by God to help others on the way.

# Life in the orchard

Life in the orchard is always interesting, and from it we can learn many things. As we grow, one tree amongst many, our branches can become entwined and entangled with others so that we claim fruit that is not our own. It can be hard to see what is us and what is someone else.

To remedy this, every so often God will take us out of the orchard and place us somewhere else. We get transplanted. This means we can see what really is us and the fruit we have produced. Often this ground is hard and unfertile. We struggle to grow in it because it isn't the nutrient-rich soil we are used to. But here we will strive to grow, pushing out roots to find the food we need. We go deeper into God. But we may not notice the growth at the time. It may not come until we are transplanted back into the fertile soil. It is here that the work that we've put in comes to fruition. The roots we have sent out readily pick up the food around us as it is plentiful. The hard times have readied us for the growing time. They are interlinked. Without the hard time our growth and productivity wouldn't be as prosperous.

Also, as we are tested in the hard ground, God is also testing the ground. As we struggle to grow there we will drop 'leaves', surplus that we can't sustain. As these fall to the ground they rot and revitalise the soil, adding nutrients to the ground. This makes the soil easier for others to grow there after we've gone. God uses us to test the ground. If we can survive there, others can as well. We are being used as pioneers. We may feel isolated, planted out on our own, but we are going on ahead of others, pushing the boundaries forward. That is if we let God transplant us and reach for Him when He places us out of reach of others.

When you plant a bamboo seed/plant there is only a small shoot to be seen for the first 4 years – why? Because it is developing its root system!  And after 4 years when a strong root system has been established the plant, in the 5th year, grows at a fantastic rate - to full height I think!

So what are we doing?

Fruit trees grow to produce fruit. We should be growing to produce our own kind of fruit. Philippians 2 calls us to hold out the bread of life to those in our generation. As trees this is what we can do. The fruit we offer to those around us can be their bread of life. But we need to make sure we manifest this fruit so that others can see it, taste it and meet God through it.

Trees support an ecosystem as they grow. Insects live there, eating what they need, using other parts to provide homes etc. The blossom produces nectar which insects eat - and also ensures pollination occurs. Imagine sitting in an orchard on a warm summers day. The sun warming all around, fruit and blossom smelling, birds singing and insects humming. It is a safe, relaxing place to be and where many enjoy being. And this, as Christians, is how we should live. We should be growing as an orchard, a place of rest and relaxation for others to experience. But is this what we are doing?

# Transplanting trees

Do you often feel unsettled about what God is doing or where you are?  But is this just God transplanting you, taking you out from where you were comfortable and placing you somewhere new, somewhere where you have to rely on him?

Do we get too secure and comfortable with where we are at?

Does this stop us reaching out and growing?

I feel that God moves us around so that we don't become settled and so that we don't become complacent. If God moves us to a different part of the orchard we will have to rely on him to give us our peace back. The change of location unsettles us, we have to search out who we are again and how we relate to those around us. We have something different inside us that we need to understand. This is God's plan so that we draw closer to him.

The new ground that God places us in may just be another area of the orchard but basically the same, or it could be a different soil make-up. We may not have the things around us that we are used to, the 'food' that we have enjoyed but rest secure in knowing that what food there is available to us is the food we need for that time. God will provide us with what we need and not let us run short. He gives us what we need to face each day if we are prepared to face the day with him. If not, we are on our own.

As land is used to grow crops etc. it loses some of its goodness. This needs to be put back and so we use artificial fertilizers so that the right nutrients are in the ground. This is only a temporary measure though. The nutrients can be washed away or leeched out by the rain, and they need replacing each year. God doesn't rely on this method to keep us well fed. He moves us to the necessary soil. It may seem to be harder work and we may not like it but it is probably a better way for us to grow.

## Why live in an orchard?

Do we need to live in an orchard, or can we be planted out on our own? What are its benefits? I believe we are in an orchard for a reason, other than that is where God has chosen to plant us!

A tree cannot live on its own. If it is on its own there is no-one to pollinate, so no fruit is produced. Trees need each other to actually live and have life. On their own they are effectively dead, like the fig tree Jesus encountered.

In the same way, for us to grow healthily and bear fruit, we need to live with others. On our own we aren't challenged to change and we don't know what we really are. We may think we are kind, patient, loving, tolerant etc. but it isn't until we are in relationships that this is actually tested. What we thought we were may be completely wrong. In His love for us, God places us with people so we can learn how to be what God asks and produce the fruit He requires. It is in interaction with others that God lovingly shows us what we really are like. If He just told us we needed to change we would be inclined to disagree, but having had the experiences we've had, God can reveal to us the changes we need to make. As the changes are revealed we are more likely to acknowledge our need for change because of the feelings the situation has provoked in us. That is if we are open to change.

So to live in an orchard allows us to become the people God created us to be.

## Whose is the fruit?

The fruit we produce isn't ours to keep. It has a purpose elsewhere. Trees produce fruit that contains seeds and the seeds are there to produce new life somewhere else. The fruit we produce is to give life to others. We can't keep hold of our fruit, that isn't its purpose and isn't healthy. Fruit left on a tree will fall to the ground and rot. Fruit kept to ourselves could lead to us becoming bitter. I'm reminded of the apple trees in "The Wizard of Oz". They became angry when Dorothy tried to take some fruit. They were bitter 'people' who wanted to keep their fruit to themselves. Is that how we want to become?


We all eat fruit because it is good for us and can be refreshing. It is a food we enjoy. As we can enjoy physical fruit, other people should be able to enjoy the fruit we produce. If we produce love, people should be able to enjoy that, along with other fruit we produce. Fruit is there for the giving, for other people's pleasure.

Also, as we give out our fruit it gives God the space to produce more of it in us. As pruning trees encourages new growth, and trees produce more fruit year on year as it is harvested, so as we give of our fruit it increases the capacity we have to hold more. If we want to love, we have to give it away. If we want to develop prophetically we have to give small words and wait for the gifting to develop. We have to give what we have to enable us to have more to give. If the basket is full God can't give us a bigger basket to hold.

## How did Jesus come?

Why did Jesus seem to break all the rules?

He touched lepers although they were considered unclean.

He healed on the Sabbath.

He forgave sins.

He didn't wash His hands before eating.

He let His disciples pick corn on the Sabbath.

He spoke to women, even to a Samaritan woman.

So why did Jesus seem to break all the rules?

He was challenging the spirit and the heart of the people,

not the rules of the book, not the rules of the system.

Do we live in freedom? Do we live from the spirit?

Or do we live in bondage to rules and laws?

## Explore the mystery

God is like a mist permeating everything.
Jesus is the centre of all things.
See Him, find Him, know Him in all things.
In all parts of each day.
In all aspects of each day.

Colossians 1:15 says
*The Son is the image of the invisible God*,
Jesus, You came and visibly expressed God
The fullness of the godhead poured into one being
and yet ... that same fullness fills the universe.
The mystery is with You

But don't let us shut down and be dismissive of the mystery
we don't comprehend.
Let us seek it, search it out and explore it.
Explore it with You as our teacher and You as our guide
Respecting what others learn on their different journey and
discovery with You.
But let us be holding dear and holding in our hearts
those things that we begin to know with You.

## Man and Woman

When God created woman He did something different.
He created the animals one by one.
He created Adam from the dust.
Each animal was a separate unit,
as was Adam at that point.
But when God created woman, He did something different.
He drew something - a rib - right out of Adam's being
and created woman around that bone.
So man and woman are unique from the rest of creation.
They are not individual separate beings - they are part of a whole
One was drawn out of the other.
They are an extension of each other.
Two parts of the same thing.
Finding their completeness in each other.
So, where in marriage we won't meld or mould or yield,
we are denying that completeness that is our real destiny,
our true potential.
To know our complete identity
we have to see it in the context of our spouse.
And the revelation of all which that means
is a constant journey of discovery.
Enjoy the journey.

## Will you fix it?

When we see something broken or out of line

in a person's life, in a situation

or in the way a group is running

our natural reaction is to want to fix it.

But maybe God doesn't actually want it fixed.

Maybe there is training in it.

Maybe there is shaping or lessons to be learnt.

Maybe it's for humbling.

If we always rush to fix it we can be in danger of

delaying the real purposes of God.

## Kingdom Living

My current understanding of this new season

is a whole new concept.

Too broad to completely understand or get a hold of.

Too fluid and flexible to explain to another.

Understood by revelation from the Father,

with on-going revelation as we walk in step with Him.

And the way forward is revealed portion-by-portion

as and when the Father wants to show us more.

He doesn't want us to get hold of His purpose

like a manual we can follow.

He doesn't want us to feel we know His agenda,

fixed and written in stone.

He wants us, always, to be looking to Him

to be listening to Him as to the next step

as to the way forward, now.

## Kingdom Living - part 2

Kingdom is a network of groups and people.
A multiplicity of relationships.
It is people gathering to share life,
to share truth of the moment,
to encourage others,
and to be encouraged themselves.
It is taking each person deeper into their relationship with the
Father

Kingdom is a building together of the people, through
relationship
and so becoming a habitation or dwelling-place
for the Father.
As He dwells within each one of us
so then He dwells throughout the Body.

It is not understood in the mind or understanding
but it is held in the spirit

It is not tied down or confined by understanding
but free to evolve, develop, and extend,
not by the hands of men
but in the hand of the Father

# Touching Heaven

Colossians 3:2 says –

*Set your minds on things above, not on earthly things*

How do we dwell more in the heavenlies?

Or set our minds on things above?

It's not a distance thing.

It's not way up there.

It's close at hand - for those who know how to access it.

Access by the spirit.

Jesus said "I am the Way."

So - walk "the way" with Jesus.

Step over  -   step into.

Touch the things of eternal value.

Live the things of eternal value.

Touch the heart of God.

Judge all things from a spiritual point of view.

Respond to all things with the heart of God

and then you have touched His heart.

Living towards others with grace and mercy

speaks of a connection with the heart of the Father.

## God's Resources

Do you worry about whether God's resources or His power

are sufficient for your situation?


Consider the small fish

who worries whether there is enough water for him to swim in

and he's in the Pacific Ocean!!


See the parallel thinking?

Craft a Word

John 14:10 in The Message Bible says
*The Father who resides in Me*
*crafts each word into a divine act.*

Doesn't it evoke such wonderful imagery
and stir your spirit?

Do you believe for your own words
to be crafted into a divine act?

They are, when, like Jesus
we speak only what we hear the Father speaking.

Ephesians 4:29 in The Passion Translation says –
*And never let ugly or hateful words come from your mouth, but*
*instead let your words become beautiful gifts that encourage*
*others; do this by speaking words of grace to help them.*

Let that be your testimony.

## Living the spiritual

I challenge myself by asking -

Am I walking in step with the Spirit ? (Gal 5:25)
Am I abiding in the Father? (John 15)
Am I hearing His words and putting them into practice?
(Matt 7:24)
Am I setting my mind on things above not on earthly things?
(Col 3:2)
Am I seeing things from His perspective, with eyes of faith
and showing grace and mercy
rather than being judgemental or condemning?
Am I knowing a life that touches and experiences the spiritual
realm as it just passes through the physical realm?
Or do I need to make some changes in some areas so that I am
more aware of the spiritual than the natural?

It's worth asking yourself the same questions.

## Who will build with me?

The following is a story to show how man has taken it into his own hands to build church how he wants to build it and not to wait for God's instructions on how He wants it built.

And a "wicker-wacker" is just a made-up name for an unknown item which represents church in the story

A certain craftsman wanted to construct a "wicker-wacker" and invited people to build with him. He advised them that the basic components included wood, fabrics, glass, coloured threads, bricks, stones and other necessary materials and that he would show them section by section how they would build.

And so the project started. People were assigned various tasks suited to their skills and things got under way, all under the direction of the craftsman. Not knowing exactly what they were building but each person being given sufficient information for their own part of the task.

However, after a short time, some people began to move off and do their own thing, starting their own projects and encouraging others to join them. They used the same materials as the others but they had no idea how to build their wicker-wacker as they didn't really know what one was. But they were full of their own ideas and wanted to do their own thing for various different reasons. Some were building fairly small projects so they were seeing quick results which satisfied their impatient natures. Others were building more slowly and more thoroughly but their flamboyant structures were getting the attention of others who were easily distracted from the original project and were caught up with the style and charisma of these structures that were taking shape more quickly than the craftsman's.

Those left on the original project were busy in their various areas. Some stitching, some building, others painting. Each focussed on the job to hand and not able to see the whole but knowing that each part and each section was important to the completion of the final thing. Some were working on site where the final assembly would be, whilst others, like those working with fabric could work wherever was suitable for them bringing each finished section to the site as and when it was ready for fitting into place. Slow steady work, but each person could be fulfilled and satisfied in what they were doing even though they couldn't see or understand the finished thing.

Whilst the work was continuing, the craftsman began to move amongst the independent projects and saw how futile their efforts were, even though some were taking great pride in what they perceived as achieving something suitable. With no understanding of what a wicker-wacker was other than a knowledge of the materials used they had gone ahead with their building not knowing shape, design or dimensions of the final thing. Although wood had been used it was beech where it should have been oak, fabrics were cotton where they should have been linen, cord where it should have been velvet, and so it went on – personal ideas but not the design of the craftsman, not a wicker-wacker at all. Design was purely of their own making – limited, small and unimaginative. Those looking for quick results were small and generally of a poor quality. Those with bigger ideas were large, flamboyant but lacking stability. None of them had constructed a wicker-wacker, and yet they mocked and scorned those workers who were still busy on the original project. Those who were faithfully working on their own section, listening to the directions from the craftsman; not knowing or understanding the complete picture but excelling in the task assigned.

And on the final day when the wicker-wacker was unveiled for all to see there were gasps of awe and amazement as its beauty and magnificence was seen for the first time. - it was truly amazing, aglow with colour, it resonated with sound, it sparkled, it was like nothing ever seen before, conceived in the mind of the craftsman who knew exactly what he was constructing and was helped by those who worked with him.

## Your Journey with God

Psalm 139:16 says -
*You saw me before I was born.*
*Every day of my life was recorded in your book.*
*Every moment was laid out before a single day had passed.*

Your journey with God is unique to you.

You can't live off the back of someone else's experience.

You have to have your own experience

and it won't be the same as other people's.

Your journey and relationship with God

is unique to you.

So know it - explore it - live it.

Live it to its full potential

and then live some more.

Define your own existence with Him

and live your life as He has purposed it since before you were

born.

Don't conform or compromise.

It's unique to you - it's exciting.

## Too big or too Small?

Where we seek to understand God
we bring Him down to our size
and that is no God at all!
We need to reach out to touch and know and explore.
We need to go further than we've gone before
but not bring Him down to our size!
If you seek to bring Him down
rather than reach out and extend your capacity,
you will never begin to touch the richness
and the fullness of all that He is and all that He has for you.
Always seeking to contain Him and to hold Him
is not the way forward.
Even when Jesus was here as a man
He was always slipping through their grasp
and leaving them confused and questioning.
We hold Him in our spirit - not our understanding.
We need, instead, to open up our whole being to receive.
If we always seek to question, rationalise, reason and understand
we won't be as rich as the one who just receives,
and lets it grow and develop by the hand of God.
Hold Him in your spirit.
Don't limit His capacity.
Continually extend your capacity to receive.

*Conversations with God*

Imagine .......
a small boy wants to talk to a fish
what would he talk about?
maybe about his bedroom; his garden or his day at school
but ......
the fish wouldn't understand
maybe about his friends; or football or TV
but ......
the fish wouldn't understand
*maybe about his holiday; his trip to the farm or his dad's new car*
but ......
the fish wouldn't understand
so
what would the fish understand?
Very little I suggest!
Maybe the fish would understand -
swimming, frogs and other fish
but not much more.
And maybe that is how it is for God when He wants to talk to us.
He has many things that He could talk about
but ..........
we wouldn't understand!
Only by the spirit can we begin to understand
the wonders of what God will share with us.
But even then there is so much more than we could manage.

## Break Open Your Word

In Psalm 119 in The Message Bible
David says  -
*Break open Your Word,*
*Let the light shine out*

The scriptures are just words on the page
unless… the Holy Spirit breaks open the word
and the light shines out
You can read 20 chapters a day
and it will do little for you
except increase your head knowledge
Or  …… you can read just one verse
and if it is broken open and
you receive revelation
it will have power.
It will feed you.
It will change you.

*Break open Your Word,*
*Let the light shine out*

## Don't despise the small things

Many things that we do or say
fan out from our lives - like a ripple effect
and we never know where they go or what they do
for good...... or for bad.


Consider the woman who packed up a lunch
gave it to her son and sent him on his way.
Did she ever know that the simple lunch she packed that day
was used to feed 5,000 people and more?
Young boys don't tell their mothers
what they've done while they've been out.
That's the way of young boys.
And it's my guess  that she never knew,
that one simple act in her daily routine
became a supernatural miracle
in the hands of Jesus.


And it's the same today - we don't know.

## Live contrary to your experience

When Jesus told Peter to go catch some fish in the daytime

It was outside of his experience.

Fish were caught at night!

It was contrary to his experience.

But because he obeyed, he had a new experience.


How often do we see or hear of Jesus doing things

that don't fit with our experience so far?

How often does He call us into things

that don't make sense?


He wants to break our mindsets; our logic;

our walking in our own understanding.

He wants us to walk in faith.

To walk in His understanding.

With eyes that see beyond the natural.

And with eyes of faith see what is happening

in the spiritual

in the heavenlies.

## Relax into the moment

Don't squeeze the life out of now
By being too busy with the next thing.

Be present to the moment.

Discipline yourself to be anchored into 'now'.

Put beauty and life into 'now'.

'Be' for the moment.

Excel in each moment.


Gal 5:25
*Since we live by the Spirit, let us keep in step with the Spirit.*

## Word or Circumstances

Psalm 46:10 says

*Be Still - and know - that I am God*

Do you allow God's word

to dictate your circumstances?

Or

do the circumstances dictate to you?

If the circumstances dictate to you

you will be blown around by them.

Feeling good when times are good.

Feeling down when times are tough.

But if you allow God's word to dictate to your circumstances

you will have His reserves of strength

to face the situations and

you will know greater peace and stillness

in your soul.

## A New Season

Many people pray for revival or a new move of God

But saints of old were known to miss God's revivals.

Why?

Because it didn't come in the form they were expecting

and so it passed them by.

God is doing a new thing right now.

Will you miss it because it doesn't fit your current mindset?

Will you miss it because it doesn't fit your current doctrine?

Will you miss it because it raises too many questions

and you can't see the answers?

Or will you hear in your spirit the fresh word of God

step out in faith and feel in a new way

the wind of the Spirit blowing through your life?

## Reality or dreams

I was reading 1 Samuel chapter 4

the incident when the Israelites lost a battle

and so they decided they needed the Ark with them to win.

However, the ark came and they still lost

and 30,00 died including Eli's sons

so having the ark didn't do anything for them.


And I considered that the ark is what God was 'contained' in

rather than God himself.

They took His container and not God into battle.


We have 'containers'

such as tradition and religion and doctrine

which we can take into situations in life

and think we are doing it with God

when in reality it's an empty box.

We need to seek God for the battles in life not just assume

that because we are taking what we think is God

that things will happen for us.

## My Journey Through Life

Let me ask myself the question ……

If I consider my life to be a spiritual journey by car……

Am I in the driving seat in control of where I go

and what route I take, making all the decisions

with God as a  passenger

involved only when I seek His advice?

Or

Is God in the driving seat taking me on His journey

following a route that He wants to take?


Who has the steering wheel  -

me or God?

## Know your Place

We are each important in God's plans and purposes.

We are important in His kingdom.

Know your place.

Know your position

and fill it  ......

to the fullness of all that God has put within you.

Eph 2:10 *For we are God's workmanship,*

*created in Christ Jesus to do good works,*

*which God prepared in advance for us to do.*

Don't neglect your good works

by giving too much time or attention

to someone else's

## Abide and Be

Have you ever noticed that the word ABIDE

is an anagram of

AID  and  BE?

So consider how, if we just learn to

ABIDE in Him

then He will  AID  us to  BE.

Not to do…… but to be.

And out of a calm place of being

we will do His doing.

So …… ABIDE  in Him

and  He will  AID  you to  BE

John 15:4-5

*Abide in Me, and I in you. As the branch cannot bear fruit of itself,
unless it abides in the vine, neither can you, unless you abide in
Me.  I am the vine, you are the branches. He who abides in Me,
and I in him, bears much fruit; for without Me you can do
nothing.*

## The Landscape of Prayer

Consider "prayer" as a place to dwell.

Consider "prayer" as a place to explore.

With its own landscape and its own features.

Trees of prayer that are bearing fruit

but also refreshing the atmosphere

as they balance the oxygen and the carbon dioxide.

Flowers bringing the beauty and fragrance of prayer.

Mountains of prayer reflecting the times of labour and struggles.

Rivers bringing refreshment and cleansing through prayer.

Homes and houses for the habitation or dwelling of prayer.

Clouds drawing up the prayers to rain down

the fruit or blessings at a later date.

Let everything become a daily journey

through the landscape of prayer,

sharing its delights as we walk and talk with

our Heavenly Father..


Rom 12:12

*Be joyful in hope, patient in affliction, faithful in prayer.*

## Prayer

Prayer is not a time for religious phrases.

Prayer is not a time for special tones of voice.

Prayer is not a time for stilted or unreal ways of communicating.

Prayer is the regular communication

and conversation between friends.

Prayer is a natural dialogue throughout the day

with our heavenly Father.

No appointment needed.

No special place.

just anytime;  anywhere


1Thess 5:17  says - *Pray continually*

## Prayer – A Labour or a Pleasure

Do I struggle

like a salmon leaping upstream

to take my prayers to God?

Or do I sit with God

at the source of the stream

and watch the answers flow down?

## Chill Out and Rest

Relax into God's love.

Know His rest.

Live the truth.

Live the freedom.

Live the moment.

Enjoyment is free,

there for the taking.

Ps 46:10

*Be still, and know that I am God; I will be exalted among the nations, I will be exalted in the earth.*

## Know Your Own Journey

Isa 25:9

*In that day they will say,*

*"Surely this is our God; we trusted in him, and he saved us.*

*This is the LORD, we trusted in Him;*

*let us rejoice and be glad in His salvation."*

We are each called to trust in our own pathway.

Not someone else's pathway but our own.

It's personal;  it's individual;

It's unique to you.

So -  know your own pathway with Him.

Trust Him in that

and see His salvation in your situations.

## Awesome Travel

Ps 104:3

*He makes the clouds his chariot*
*and rides on the wings of the wind.*

What an awesome way to travel!
Much better than the bus or the train.

Will I get to travel like that one day?

All things are possible with God!

Don't limit your expectations
Especially when it comes to what we might do
in eternity.

Book a cloud now so you won't be disappointed!
It might be your chariot one day!

### The 2½ Tribes

When the Children of Israel went into the Promised Land
2½ tribes said "No thank you, we'd rather stay here"
On the edge - just outside.
Satisfied with something less than the full blessing
God had in mind for His people.


Are we in danger of being like those 2½ tribes?
Settling with something less than God's new season.
Staying with the familiar, with what we know and understand,
rather than crossing over in faith.
Rather than entering into the new season of what God is doing
today.
A fresh wind is blowing from the heavenlies.
Will you set your sail to let it take you
on His chosen path
or will you choose to row with self effort on the course
you have set and planned?

## Relationship or requests

What is prayer all about - relationship or requests?

Surely it has to be about relationship first?

Relationship first and foremost.

For it is only out of relationship we can know

God's heart and mind.

And if prayer is praying into being those things

that are on the heart and mind of God,

then we have to have the relationship

that hears and knows His heart and mind.


John 5:19

*Jesus gave them this answer: "I tell you the truth, the Son can do*

*nothing by himself; he can do only what he sees his Father doing,*

*because whatever the Father does the Son also does.*

## Changes and Choices

2 Cor 3:18 says -

*And we are being transformed into his likeness*

*with ever-increasing glory,*

*which comes from the Lord, who is the Spirit.*

He does the changing  -  we can't

But ......

We make the choices  -  He can't

What choices are you making?

## The Silent Pathway

Are you walking a spiritual journey

that hasn't yet found its physical expression?


Don't be discouraged by the lack of tangible markers

but live it to the fullness of the revelation

that you have been given so far.


God will break it open into the physical......

in His time.

## Thoughts from the Father

Go out there and walk the landscape.

The landscape of God's Kingdom.

Tread the pathways of wisdom, understanding and knowledge.

Pass through the doorways and step into a new experience

with your Heavenly Father.

Step into a new realm of life and understanding.

Don't think ......

but reach out and feel and touch.

Don't think ......

but draw in, breathe in and absorb.

Absorb from the realm of light and truth.

Don't think ......

But receive impartation, receive revelation,

not rational thought or thinking.

But open up the mind, open up the spirit

and receive the thoughts of the Father

and in its time...... it will surface in the mind

as wisdom and understanding.

## Trust in the Father

Trust in the Father ......for all things

and live in peace and stillness of the soul.

Keep company with the Trinity ......

Father, Son and Holy Spirit.

For ...in His presence is fullness of joy

Don't let thoughts of today consume your thinking.

Don't let concerns of tomorrow dominate your mind.

Don't get caught up with daily life.

Get caught up with Him.

Step into Him.

Reach through into the spiritual

and bring to the natural

what you find in the spiritual.

## Rules and Methods

I read that the desire for rigid doctrine

is in direct proportion

to our inability to actually hear His voice.


Quite a statement  -  but seems quite true


How much easier it is to know the rules,

to know the method,

to know what's expected

rather than to hear what the Father would say

about each and every situation.

But ...... rules and method are religion.

Hearing Father is life and Kingdom

## What Atmosphere Do I Create

With our speech

we design and alter our environment

for good or for bad.


So when the atmosphere is not comfortable,

and when there is tension in the air

how did it get like that?

Consider - what have I said in the last while

that is making the environment a more hostile place?


Eph 4:29

*Do not let any unwholesome talk come out of your mouths, but*

*only what is helpful for building others up according to their*

*needs, that it may benefit those who listen.*

Or as it says in The Passion Translation

*Let your words become beautiful gifts*

*that encourage others*

*do this by speaking words of grace to help them*

## Knowledge or Revelation?

The world likes success and achievement.

But, becoming an expert in an area of scripture

is the very thing that closes us off

from learning the new things

that God is opening up in His Word.


We live by revelation  -  from the Father,

not information  -  from people, books, sermons.

As it says in Colossians 2:3 (Passion Translation)

*For our spiritual wealth is in Christ,*

*like hidden treasure waiting to be discovered—*

*heaven's wisdom and endless riches of revelation knowledge.*

Don't seek "knowledge."

The world seeks knowledge.

Seek truth and revelation in Christ.

## I AM

Exodus 3:14 says.......

I AM who I AM

or

I WILL BE what I WILL BE.

Implying ...... don't make me something else.

Don't make Me fit your narrow mindset.

We need to allow Him to be God

and not seek to define Him by ....

our limited understanding.

We need to allow Him to be God

and not expect Him to perform ......

as we want Him to perform.

He's bigger than all of that

and we will know more of His character

and more of His power

if we let Him be what He will be.

## Why?

It's no sin to ask God

"Why?"

But can we handle the answers?


The bigness of God

is always bigger

than our question

"Why?"


Isa 48:17

*I am the LORD your God,*

*who teaches you what is best for you,*

*who directs you in the way you should go.*

## A Friend Prayed

One evening a friend prayed …..

"Father … as we sleep go ahead of us into tomorrow"

and it just caught my imagination and I considered how

perhaps

God wants us to sleep each night

so that …..

He can get on with planning tomorrow

without us interfering.

And so … we awake to a day prepared by Him.

Every part planned and organised.

Every provision made.

He has gone ahead …..

and prepared the day for us.

Live it and walk it with Him.

## Commissions from God

If God gives us a commission

then He resources that commission.

It may sometimes feel like a treasure hunt

......searching for clues

as to where the next portion is.

But if it is His commission

He has resourced it and it will happen


Consider Hebrews 11:33

(Passion Translation)

*Their faith fastened onto their promises*

*and pulled them into reality*

So ...... if God has commissioned you with something

be like the saints of old

and by faith pull it into reality,

seeing God equip and resource for what is needed.

## Seeing Him who is invisible

Are you walking a spiritual journey that hasn't yet found

it's physical expression in this place?

So do you struggle sometimes when the way looks bleak

and there is no fruit from what you do?

Do you struggle when there is no evidence

of what you believe God has spoken?

Then consider the many in Hebrews 11

who walked a similar way.

They were carrying something in their heart

but never seeing the fulfilment.

And be like Moses in verse 27

where it says

*Moses kept right on going*

*because ………*

*He kept his eyes on the One who is invisible.*

Keep your eyes on the One who is invisible

and you will have hope and strength to keep on going.

<u>The reality of sin</u>

Sin is not wrong <u>doing.</u>

Sin it is wrong <u>being.</u>

It's not rooted in what we do.

It's rooted in the essence of our very being.

It is seen through what we do,

but is integral to who we are.

## More than Conquerors

Being more than conquerors means that ......

we not only conquer but ......

we accept the situation as an opportunity

to walk further and deeper with God.

## Faith

Faith isn't the ability to believe
long and far into the misty future
It's simply taking God at His word
and taking the next step.
Faith is pulled out of the abstract
and lived with the concrete certainty
in the here and now.

Mark 4:24 and 25

*Then Jesus added,*
*Pay close attention to what you hear.*
*The closer you listen,*
*the more understanding you will be given*
*and you will receive even more.*
*To those who listen to my teaching,*
*more understanding will be given.*
*But for those who are not listening,*
*even what little understanding they have*
*will be taken away from them.*
And in Luke 6 Jesus tells us that
those who hear His teachings and put them into action
are building a strong foundation in their life.
A life that will survive the storms and challenges of life.
But those who hear His teachings
and don't put them into action will have a weak foundation
which will give way when life's challenges come.
Are you taking action with what you hear?
Are you taking action with what you read?
Is your foundation strong enough for life's storms?

## The World Beyond

Do you hear advance echoes of the world beyond?

What is going on beyond?

What can I see; what can I hear

if I use my spiritual eyes and ears?

What are the deeper mysteries of the kingdom?


John 16:15 says

*The Spirit will take from what is mine*

*and make it known to you.*


That is where or how we will hear

"the advance echoes of the world beyond"

Let the Spirit speak the mysteries of God to you.

## Answers –v- Solutions

In the kingdom

There aren't many answers

But there are many solutions

<u>God is love</u>

The key element of kingdom living is ......

"Love."

God is love.

He doesn't do love.

He is love.


And that is what He wants from us in this world.

Not a people who "do" love.

But a people who "are" love.

So that we are love towards every person.

We are love towards every situation.

Love is our very nature.

## God's Ambassadors

Enter each day as God's messenger.

As His ambassador to a dark world

that knows little of Him.

Carrying His presence or His purpose

to everyone we meet.

Being the representation of God

to a people who don't yet know Him.

As Jesus said to Philip in John 14:9

*Anyone who has seen Me has seen the Father.*

And so it should be for us.

Anyone who has seen me

should have seen the Father.

We should live a life and be a people

who are a visible representation of God

to a people who don't yet know Him.

## At Night

At night ......

The day is spent!

How have I <u>spent</u> the time?

We give a lot of thought to how we spend our money.

Do we give the same thought to how we spend our time?

Keep in step with the Spirit

Galatians 5:25 says

*Since we are living by the Spirit,*

*let us follow the Spirit's leading*

*in every part of our lives.*

That says it all really!

## Praying for Another

When I pray for another person

I should be asking God to open my eyes

so that I can see that person

as He does.

And then I should enter into the stream of love

that He already directs towards them

or

enter into an understanding of what

He is doing with that person.

And then I can pray in-line with what He is doing.

## Dealing with the Storm

As I watched the bird flying in the strong wind

that was blowing that day,

I saw how effortlessly it was moving through the sky

as it allowed the storm to carry it.

It rode with the wind

and went where the storm took it

with less effort than when it flew on a quieter day.

If it had sought to do different,

it would have had a mighty struggle.

But in yielding to the storm

it took advantage of what was there.

How differently we respond to the winds of life.

We often resist and become weary in the struggle,

discouraged as we fight.

But we should consider the options.....

and having considered the strength of the storm

we can yield to it, go with it and let it carry you.

Or we can choose to seek shelter in the Rock

and wait until it passes.

Or like some birds – we can face the wind

and seek to gain altitude

getting ever closer to the Son

I am the Way

Maps and guidebooks are fine,
but when the sky grows dark
and the path gets rough,
and the mist comes down – what then?
And it's the same when life becomes a struggle
and we don't know which way to turn
our best resource is the Guide, Himself

Isa 50:10 says -
*Let him who walks in the dark,*
*who has no light,*
*trust in the name of the LORD*
*and rely on his God.*

Know your Guide and let Him take you through the dark times.

# God is responsible

Remember that it is God who is responsible for everybody.

He is responsible for everything  ……  not you.

You are only responsible for those people

that God asks you to do something for.

He will look after the others in a different way.

If you forget this, you will become weary

and fall into a place without peace.

Many people demand that you look after them.

Do not respond to them unless the Holy Spirit talks to you.

He will take you to the people and places you need to go.

Jesus passed many people who were needy but did not talk to

them when He walked through Israel.

He just walked on by.

In some places He did no miracles at all.

He looked for faith

and for people who were wanting to move into His Kingdom.

Desperate people do not always have faith.

They are desperate because they do not have faith.

Continue to grow in your listening and obedience to the Holy

Spirit and reach those people He wants you to reach.

Leave the rest to Him.

## God does not forget us

A man was shipwrecked on a desert island.

He built himself a hu.t

The days were hot - the nights were cold

He scanned the horizon for ships day after day

but none passed by.

One day he returned from wandering the island

and found his hut burnt to the ground

a smoking heap of ashes - he had nothing left!

He was distraught as he lay beside the ruins and slept.

Next morning he woke to find a ship anchored off the island.

As the captain approached, he said

"We saw your smoke signal and came to rescue you!"

All the man possessed had to be destroyed

before he could be found and rescued.

God had seemed so distant – for so long.

But He was working on both ends of the situation.

To bring the rescue ship near at just the right time

and to reduce the marooned man to nothing

in order to bring him to his knees.

Does this speak something into your life right now?

## Revelation

God wants to reveal things to us that have no corresponding

earthly picture.

But we have to be willing to receive things into our spirit

that don't seem logical or rational,

that we can't understand with our minds.

But we know that we have seen something from God.

How can we receive His mysteries

if we will only consider those things that we understand with our

mind?


John 16:15

*The Spirit will take from what is mine*

*and make it known to you.*

## The Spiritual world

The spiritual world is not merely adjacent to the visible world

but it fills it right through,

and we need to know how to touch it

more readily.

How to explore it

and appropriate what we find there.

And only the Spirit can reveal that to us.

---

# Truth or theory

Truths that are not experienced are theories, not truths.

So do a check and consider -

Do I only have theory and sound ideas in my life

or do I have experience of these things

so they are built into the very fabric of my being?


For example  -  God is my Provider ...

do I experience His provision when a dry time comes my way

or do I only know poverty and debt when finance is short.


God gives peace as a gift  ......

Do I know how to receive that peace

or step into that place of peace

or is my experience worry and fretting and sleepless nights?


Truth or theory .....   what do I have?

and so ... what do I give to others?

It is only "truth" that brings freedom to myself or others

## Revealed

God is bigger than His book .

The Bible does not contain Him,

it reveals Him.

Don't limit yourself or confine yourself but

explore the limitless experience

and understanding of God.

## The Father's Favour

Do we try to obtain the Father's favour

through our labours

rather than working from a place of favour?

His favour is upon us because He loves us

not because of what we do for Him.

So know yourself in that place of favour

and then step out from there.

Step into that place of acceptance and favour

and from there do what He calls you to do.

Know that He wants the depths of our hearts

not the religious deeds of our hands.

<u>John 14:21</u>

*He who loves Me will be loved by My Father*
*and I too will love him and show myself to him.*

God reveals Himself to those who love Him.
He isn't concerned about the mistakes along the way
as much as ……
a heart that seeks after Him; a heart that loves Him,
and a heart that lives from faith
It's the condition of our heart that is important
not our actions – whether good or bad by our estimation.
That is why David was acceptable to God.
He wasn't alienated because of his misdeeds.
He was embraced because of his good heart.
People will too quickly examine your deeds and judge you
accordingly.
But God examines the heart
and reveals Himself to those who love Him.

## Grace Be With You

At the end of every Epistle Paul says –

*Grace be with you*

Or ........

*Grace be with your spirit.*

Does this mean ......

May you experience God's grace in your life?

Or does it mean ......

may grace be part of your nature, part of your make-up

so that you readily show grace and mercy to others

rather than judgement?

Or does it mean something of both?

Grace

Eph 4:7 says -

*But to each one of us <u>grace has been given</u> as*
*Christ apportioned it*

So consider - How do we use that grace?
Or do we more easily come in with judgement?

Jesus showed grace to the Samaritan Woman
and the whole village came out to hear Him
and many believed in Him.
But what would we do today?
It is much more likely
that she would have been judged by the church
and the whole village would have turned away from God.

Grace or judgement?
It's a serious consideration

## My Faith

It's not a religion to be compared with other religions.

It can't be defined by rules and doctrines and teachings.

Although, traditionally, that is what has happened.

It's a friendship; it's a relationship with God.

It's a journey with Him.

A growing changing lifestyle shaped by Him.

And it's different for everyone.

We can't prescribe to others how their relationship should be

because it's individual and personal,

dependent on what He has invested in us.

It's dependent on how we each fit into His eternal plan.

It's not a set of rules or beliefs

It's a relationship to be lived.

## Robbed or Mis-used

When the Israelites left Egypt they carried great riches.

Gold, silver and jewels which their Egyptian neighbours had given.

God's plan for this wealth was for the people to build Him a dwelling place so He could live in the midst of the people.

But in Exodus 32 satan tempts them to use these same riches to build an idol.

And they build a golden calf out of the gold which they then worship!

How often does satan try and steal the riches God gives us today and use them for his own ends?

How often do we lose what God has invested in us because we have let satan rob us?

And like the Israelites we can end up worshipping the gift not the Giver!!

Satan uses the same strategies today

Beware of the wiles of the evil one

Are we seeing God's current revelation?


John 5:16

*So, because Jesus was doing these things (healing)*

*on the Sabbath, the Jews persecuted him.*


The Pharisees were so concerned

about the details of the law

that they missed the revelation

that stood among them!


How much are we at risk at getting caught up with the

incidentals of church life and church busyness

So that we miss what God is doing or saying right now?

## Good Morning !!

Good Morning!

This is God

Just wanting to let you know

I will be handling all

of your problems today.

I <u>will not</u> need your help

So relax ...... and have a

Good Day!

## How Real is Your Relationship

I need to know Christ as my centre.

Even at my lowest point.

Or in my darkest times.

Otherwise ......

there is no reality in my relationship with Him

I need to be like David who could say


Ps 16:8

*I have set the LORD always before me.*

*Because he is at my right hand, I shall not be shaken.*

## Don't let the enemy destroy your Marriage

As seen in Eph 5 marriage is a reflection of

Christ and the Church.

And the enemy hates Christ and the church

so for that reason he hates marriage

and seeks to destroy it.

Marriage should be our richest, strongest

and most pleasurable relationship.

Yet for many it is a place of distress, abuse

or at best – quiet resignation.

But I say - fight for your marriage.

Go on the attack.

Make it the treasure in your life that it ought to be.

But ... don't focus on your partner

and the failings you might see in that area.

Focus on the enemy and fight where the real battle is.

Solomon's Wisdom

1Kings 4 tells us that
*God gave Solomon wisdom and very great insight,*
*and a breadth of understanding*
*as measureless as the sand on the seashore.*

*His wisdom was greater than the wisdom*
*of all the men of the East,*
*and greater than all the wisdom of Egypt.*

*He was wiser than any other man,*
*And his fame spread to all the surrounding nations.*

*He spoke three thousand proverbs*
*and his songs numbered a thousand and five.*

*He described plant life,*
*from the cedar of Lebanon*
*to the hyssop that grows out of walls.*
*He also taught about animals and birds, reptiles and fish.*

*Men of all nations came to listen to Solomon's wisdom,*
*sent by all the kings of the world,*
*who had heard of his wisdom.*

Who needs university or knowledge when God can do this?
Jeremiah 33:3 says
*Call unto Me and I will answer you*
*and tell you great and unsearchable things*
*that you do not know*
He is still the same God today,
but what He does, He does for a purpose
not just to make us look smart

<u>Servant or Friend?</u>

In John 15:15 Jesus told His disciples

they were no longer servants

…….. but friends.

Servants are task-orientated.

Friends are relationship orientated.

Servants don't know what the master thinks.

Friends do know what the master thinks.

Servants work <u>for</u> Him.

Friends work <u>with</u> Him.

Too many people live as servants of God

and not as friends of God.

Check your own position and

live the relationship God wants with you.

## Resistance to change

Resistance to change

is a resistance to the nature of God.

He is always doing a new thing.

Always creative and doing things in a fresh way.

As when Jesus healed people when He was here,

it was different every time.

He doesn't want us to hold fast to tradition or doctrine,

but to be willing to let go when He speaks something different.

He doesn't want us to learn "how to ….."

and learn method.

He wants us to learn "how to listen to His voice"

in every situation,

because He enjoys communing with us.

He doesn't want us in bondage to our doctrines,

traditions or programmes

so that we won't change when He says

"Let us do it this way now."

## Don't settle for the wrong thing

When the Wise Men followed the star

they got as far as Jerusalem … and the palace of Herod

and believed they had reached their destination.

The situation met their expectations

as to where they expected to find a new king.

But ….. it was not the place.

It was not a palace in Jerusalem

but a stable in Bethlehem where Jesus was found.

And I was seeing a parallel in our perception of church today

Many have settled for a "Jerusalem"

Church with leaders and programmes and agendas

But God wants us to find the "Bethlehem"

The unstructured, God-led

relationship and network-based kingdom living

## Faith

What is the opposite of faith?

Doubt ?

Or is it certainty?

It's worth thinking about isn't it?

When we are certain of the way

it doesn't require faith.

So sometimes the opposite of faith ....

is certainty.

And sometimes when we feel we are doubting,

the truth is we are just feeling vulnerable

as we walk in an area of faith.

And walking in faith is a good place to be.

## His Purposes

Be a people   ........

who call forth His purposes.


A people who hear His heart

A people who know His mind

A people who listen to His voice


And ......


Be a people   ........

who call forth His purposes.

So that His will, will be done, on earth

as it is in heaven.

## Dreaming

Is God still dreaming and planning .....

Or is He watching His original dream

play itself out day-by-day?

Interesting thought!

## Courage

Courage is not the absence of fear.

Rather ……

It is choosing to act in spite of the fear.

## Communication with God

If God rarely speaks to us in an audible, tangible way

why do we, as people, primarily speak with Him in that way?

Why do we use the medium of verbal communication.

We need to be much more creative

in how we communicate with Father

and in the process ......

we may find .....

we more easily hear Him ....

in non-verbal communication.

We will become more aware of

His mediums of communication ....

as we explore them ourselves.

## True Stillness

Sometimes we deceive ourselves into thinking

we have inner peace

when the truth is  .........

we have quiet tension.

And that is not trust

but simply compressed anxiety.

## The Power of Inner Peace

When we truly have inner peace

resulting in stillness in our soul.

When we fully trust

then God's power and purpose is released

more readily into our situation.

Inner peace releases power.

That is why the enemy seeks to rob us of our peace,

through worry, stress and anxiety.

He wants to keep us in that weaker place.

Resist the enemy and maintain your peace.

Experience the power released when we live

from inner and stillness.

## At Rest

When things are allowed to rest

or settle.........

It is then that they find their natural place.

So ..... rest in Him and find your natural place.

## At Peace

Ecclesiastes 4:6 says

*Better one handful with tranquillity*

*(stillness or peace)*

*Than two handfuls with toil*

*and chasing after the wind.*

Modern living encourages the latter

at the expense of the former.

Modern living causes us to chase the wind

Rather than have stillness in my soul.

It's my responsibility to make right choices

in how I choose to live.

Will I go with the values of the world and all the hassle that

brings

or with the values of the kingdom

and an inner peace?

## Chill Out

Proverbs 20:24 says ......

*The LORD directs our steps,*

*so why try to understand everything along the way?*


Proverbs 19:21 says .....

*You can make many plans,*

*but the LORD's purpose will prevail.*


It's true.

So why do we try and understand it all?

Chill out and

just walk where He takes you

## God is Unlimited

Don't look at life's difficulties,

challenges and problems

from your own limitations.

Rather ….

See them from the unlimited

powers of Heaven.

Reach out to God in faith

and expect to be surprised

by what He will do.

Don't draw on your meagre resources

But draw on His abundant resources.

Live from the truth of Ephesians 3:20


*Now to him who is able to do immeasurably more than all we*

*ask or imagine, according to his power that is at work within*

*us,  to him be glory in the church and in Christ Jesus throughout*

*all generations, for ever and ever! Amen.*

## Entrenched

It is possible to become "entrenched"

in an old model of church

(where entrenched means -

established firmly or dug in)

It's possible to believe its hundreds of years of history

makes it right

But at its worst it has a testimony of hypocrisy,

division, abuse, war,

intolerance and control

greater than any testimony it professes of

love and grace.


Are you entrenched in something

that has passed its sell-by date?

Or have you heard the call of God

to a new season – to where He is at today?

## Supple and Capacious

In the introduction to the Book of Romans

In The Message Bible it says –

*Paul's mind was supple and capacious!*

What an amazing phrase!

Supple to God and all He says.

Capacious to receive

as much as God will give.

I hope the same is true of me.

## Hearing God

Oswald Chambers suggests that we need to be devoted to

listening if we want to hear God more easily

and more regularly.

He suggests that our inability to hear God

is the result of our giving attention to other things.

We only hear God at certain times

because the rest of the time

we give our attention to other things.

Our minds and our beings are involved elsewhere

and we are not devoted to listening.

We need to develop.......

A devotion to listening.

## Confusion of Babylon

When man tried to reach God through self effort

by building the Tower of Babel,

languages confused and divided people.

In recent times

when man has built a hierarchical system of church

and tries to reach God through self effort,

doctrine confuses and divides people.

Find God where He is working today

And walk with Him there.

## Who is our Teacher?

We have emphasised the Bible

and the Sunday morning teaching

to the neglect of the teaching from the Spirit.

as in 1 John 2:27 where it says –

*But you have received the Holy Spirit, and he lives within you, so*

*you don't need anyone to teach you what is true. For the Spirit*

*teaches you everything you need to know, and what he teaches is*

*true—it is not a lie.*

The teaching from the Spirit will always be

personal to me and my journey.

It will be pertinent to the moment

because He knows where I am at right now

and where I am going.

He knows what I am resisting

and what I need to embrace.

His teaching is personal and will impact my life.

## Echoes of the Father

As an echo has no voice of its own

but repeats what another has said, so,

in the same way

we should be an echo of the Father.

WE should be only speaking what we have heard the Father

speak

As in John 16:13where it says

*When the Holy Spirit comes*

*He will not speak on His own but …*

*He will speak only what He hears from the Father.*

What better model

What better example can we have

than to be like the Holy Spirit?

Become an echo and bring the living word of God

Reflecting Jesus

As the image in a mirror has no substance of its own

but merely reflects the image that is before it

so we should have nothing of ourselves

but be a reflection of all that is in Jesus.

But this is not done by self-effort.

It is done by a work of God in our lives.

For it says in 1 Corinthians 3:18

*We who reflect the Lord's glory*

*are being transformed into His likeness*

*with ever-increasing glory*

*which comes from the Lord –*

*who is the Spirit*

## God Awareness 24/7

Oswald Chambers suggests that

the busyness of things

obscures our concentration on God.

It is an on-going challenge in our 21st century lives

to maintain a position of beholding Him.

But we should never let a hurried lifestyle

disturb the relationship of –

abiding in Him.

And in that place of abiding we will find

our souls are restored

our focus is clear

and our stress levels will be reduced.

## Rooted in Jesus

Colossians 2:7 encourages us to have our lives rooted in Jesus.

And if we truly are rooted in Him,

drawing life and nourishment from

the River of Life then

we won't know healing -by- healing

but we will know health.

We won't know need-by-need being met

but we will know provision.

It's the difference between using a battery

or

being connected to the source of the power.

## Rooted in Jesus - 2

Whatever we are rooted in

will determine how we grow

or whether we grow.

A hydrangea plant produces pink flowers

when it is grown in one type of soil

and

it produces blue flowers

when it is grown in another type of soil.

What it is rooted in affects what it grows and produces.

What we are rooted in will affect who we are

and how we grow.

So  …. if we are rooted in Christ

we will produce the fruit of the Spirit

as in Galatians 5:21.

But if we are rooted in the things of the world

It will be evident in what our lives produce.

## Power of God

We should be living more in the power of God

Rather than in our own strength.

Then we would see more of the miraculous.

But consider .......

He doesn't see these acts of power as miraculous,

they're just normal events to Him,

just what He does.

We consider things to be miraculous

because they happen outside the laws of life,

outside the rules of living as we know them.

Yet we should be living beyond those laws of life

and be living the principles of the Kingdom.

Then we wouldn't be "wowed" by what happened

and we would be more expectant

for these acts of power to be happening.

WHappening whenever and wherever God is moving.

Not doubting but expectant.

## God Loves Me

Yes ...... God loves me.

Not because of who I am.

Not because of what I do.

Not because of how pleasing I am to Him.


No ......


God loves me ......

Because of who He is.

And He IS love.

And that will never change.

And He will always love me.

## The Growth of the Kingdom

This is the beginning of a new age.

The beginning of the age of the Kingdom.

As the man-centred Church struggles to go forward it will

struggle with man's effort.

But the Kingdom of God will grow and spread –

slowly, quietly and unseen

yet influencing many things.

It will grow in strength as God pours His Spirit through the

network.

Unseen and silent to those who are blind

but powerful and strong as God's favour

prospers the work of His hand.

And it will not be self-effort, toil and labour

raising up the proud and crushing the poor

but it will be a Kingdom where all things are equal,

all people are equal.

And through relationship they will care for one another.

They will be lifting up one another.

They will be encouraging one another.

And there will be a strength and a power that has not been seen

for many years so .....

Arise …… shine …….

for the light has come.

The feet of the messenger are heard coming over the mountains

as he brings the message of hope and a future.

Like John the Baptist of old there is a

Closing of the door on an old order and …..

ushering in the new.

And God's glory will be seen in that place.

God's glory will be seen throughout the world.

In a Kingdom of righteousness peace and joy.

So .......

God loves me ......
because of who He is
So ......
It's not dependent on me at all
but ......
on His faithfulness and covenant – keeping nature
and so ......
all our situations and circumstances
should be viewed from that perspective.

How is God's love for me seen
in this situation?
How is God's love for me seen
in every situation?
It's easier to walk the tough times
when we allow God's love to wrap around them.
But the choice is ours.
Don't let your questions, doubts or frustrations
rob you of the peace that His love brings.

## Misunderstanding

Mis-understanding means ......

we have missed the understanding

from His perspective.

We so easily forget that our understanding

is flawed by our fleshly thinking

and that

His understanding is powered by faith.

<u>Doctrine</u>

Doctrine ......

Is man's attempt to define God and His ways.


And God isn't to be defined

or confined by man.


God is I AM.

I AM what I will be.

Not what man tells Him to be.

## Osmosis

Osmosis is the passage of water from a region of high water
concentration through a semi-permeable membrane to a region
of low water concentration

Or

The fuller passes to the lesser / drier

So ........

As I sit with God ......

His fullness just filters into my dryness / emptiness

and fills me up

as I soak in Him

His life ..... just flows into me

as I rest in His presence.

## Acts of Power

We may wonder why we don't see as many

"acts of power" as the apostles did.

But …… may I suggest that

we need to be more sensitive to God's timing,

more aware of God's involvement.

May I suggest that we too easily move

ahead of time

and go forth in self effort

fuelled by emotions or good intentions.

Jesus was always patient and said ….. He only did

what He saw His Father doing.

And so ….. when His mother asked Him

to help at the wedding when they ran out of wine,

He didn't act immediately.

He waited until He knew God's involvement

in the situation.

When He heard Lazarus was ill

He didn't act immediately.

He waited until He saw God raising from the dead

rather than healing.

Can we have the patience to wait on God's timing?

To know God's involvement and see more acts of power?

## Entrenched

Many people have become entrenched

in the wrong model of church

Believing that its hundreds of years of history

makes it right.

The only thing that makes anything right

Is the breath of God blowing through it.

The only thing that makes anything right

is the Word of God speaking into it.

The only thing that makes anything right

is the will of God for each day

Gal 5:25

*Let us keep in step with the Spirit.*

Not the ways of man.

## Bricks or Seeds

How do I relate to others?

Do I drop bricks into people's lives

by criticising; judging; discouraging?

Or

Do I sow seeds into people's lives?

Do I sow seeds of life; seeds of truth

seeds of encouragement?

Bricks destroy and crush people.

Seeds bring forth fruit and a good harvest

So – don't drop bricks

But ......

Sow seeds and watch them bear fruit.

## A Gift

When I was born God put something into my hand

into my heart  ……

He put a gift for me to use

in whatever way I choose.

The gift?

……… a life.

To do with as I choose.

So how do I choose to use that life?

Do I have my own plans; my own agendas

my own ways,

that I ask Him to smile on and bless?

Or have I handed that life back to Him

and said I am Yours.

Use me in whatever way You want to

to fulfil the eternal plans in Your heart.

Let me be a part of what You are doing

and not ask You to be a part of what I am doing.

## To do His Will

We sometimes live our lives as if ……

Jesus is there to assist us in our labours

rather than …….

us do His bidding.

Our labours of self efforet will eventually be burnt up

like wood, hay and straw

(1 Corinthians 3)

so why labour in vain?

His bidding will become as treasure

laid up in heaven as a firm foundation

for us, in the coming age

(1 Timothy 6)

## Prayer

The deeper place of prayer

Is to hear the heart of God

and to pray it into being.

His will heard from heaven

and brought to earth.

That is effective prayer.

That is prayer that will make a difference.

His nature or mine?

Many of us develop our Christian lives

along the lines of our own nature

rather than

along the lines of God's nature.

But there is hope in 2 Cor 3:18

for ...... if we are willing

He is wanting to transform us into His image.

## Walking in Wisdom

When we walk in wisdom

we mirror the reality of heaven

here on earth.

## Kingdom Currency

The currency of the world

is money

but ......

the currency of the Kingdom

is faith...

What currency are you most familiar with?

Kingdom –v- World

Are we seeking to change the world

Or

Are we seeking to see a stronger Kingdom established?

Are we building into that Kingdom day-by-day?

For that is what will change the world

## Delayed Answers to Prayer

Might I suggest -

Delayed answers to prayer ......

are not refusals necessarily.

Many prayers are received and recorded

with a note saying

"My time has not yet come"

## A Restless Place

Is your mind a restless place?

Do you have thoughts flitting here and there

darting around your mind in a random fashion?

Does it have no focus; no control; no discipline?

Is it a restless place?

Rest – less  hhmmm!

If we know His peace and rest in our lives

and in our mind

then we will know it as a restful place.

It will be a place with harmony and pattern,

focussed thoughts

and a place of stillness

A place where Christ enjoys to dwell.

Rather than a place where He is bombarded

with an overload of erratic thoughts.

BE STILL  - and know …… that He is God

## Death

Death .......

Removes people from this sphere of existence.

For a Christian ......

no illness is terminal

because ......

terminal means .... the end of the line!

whereas ....

for a Christian

it's just a point of transition.

It's just a point of exchange.

## Christ in the World

Christ lives in me

and wants to be evident through my life.

He wants to be seen by …. what I do and how I live.

He wants to be manifest through me …..

to the world.

So I need to yield to Him.

I need to submit to His plans.

I need to hear what He is saying

and to respond and obey.

So that …. I will be

the visible image

of the invisible God

## What matters?

To the people of faith in Hebrews 11
the things that are not seen mattered more to them
than the things that are seen.
2 Cor 4:18 tell us that the things that are seen
are temporal
but the things which are not seen are eternal
So pray – as in Eph 1 –
That the eyes of your heart be enlightened
so that you will see more of the unseen things of God
the things which are of eternal value.

## Consider

Consider the thought .......

While God will not go against ...

His word.

He will often go against ...

our understanding of His Word.

He wants to take us into the fullness of His thinking

not the narrowness of our own thinking.

But we have to be willing to yield our logic and rationale

sometimes.

## Music

Music creates or takes us to

another dimension.

It is a tool or channel for something more.

Something of a spiritual dimension.

So that .....

sometimes as we listen to it,

we become less aware of the music

and more aware of the spiritual dimension

that it has taken us to.

It carries the echo of another world.

Do you hear it?

## Relationship with God

Why? ...... has the relationship with God

become a system; an institution; an organisation

with doctrines; agendas; mission statements

so defined; proscribed; rational and mind-based?

Jesus died .......

to restore relationship with the Father

so ......

Why?  has the relationship with God

become a system;

Because men like to be in control.

Are we walking or willing to walk

where God is fully in control.

## Where am I living from?

Living from myself .......

causes me to be brought down

by my own inadequacies; concerns and anxieties.

Living from within .......

from the Spirit

or from God's fullness within me

connects me to all of Him

that is invested in me.

And in that place ....

all things are possible.

Phil 4:13

*I can do everything through him who gives me strength.*

## God ways -vs- Secular ways

Few people take their problems first to God.

Instead we go to the secular places of "wisdom".

If we have a cold ….

the first place we go is the doctor's surgery.

If we need money ……

the bank will give a loan.

Whatever the problem

there is a secular answer,

that offers instant solutions

rather than the patient waiting on God.

God uses many problems in our lives

in order to mould us into a unique shape.

We create a different shape from His desired option

by finding our secular answers.

## Do You Know?

Do you know that you were carefully and lovingly made?

That the Father put within you all that He wanted

to satisfy Himself and Jesus in that portion of His creation.

That you are what you are because He desires to enjoy

what you are.

And that when He made you, He looked .....

and He saw .....

that it was good.

So live in His delight of you and rejoice with Him.

## Creativity

God is a God of creativity.

From the very beginning ...... from creation

until now..... and to the end where there is no end.

It is His nature,

and ..... we are made in His image.

So ........ creativity is in our nature.

But do we give it room for expression?

Do we walk in creativity?

Or do we walk in ...... predictability?

Creativity is the ability to transcend traditional ideas,

rules and patterns

and to create meaningful new ideas or interpretations.

Creativity is to live from revelation and insight.

Predictability is the antithesis of creativity.

# Waiting for Jesus

John 6:16-21 says -

*That evening Jesus' disciples went down to the shore*

*to wait for him.*

*But as darkness fell and Jesus still hadn't come back,*

*they got into the boat and headed across the lake toward*

*Capernaum.*

*Soon a gale swept down upon them,*

*and the sea grew very rough.*

*They had rowed three or four miles when suddenly*

*they saw Jesus walking on the water toward the boat.*

*They were terrified,*

*but he called out to them, "Don't be afraid. I am here!*

*Then they were eager to let him in the boat,*

*and immediately they arrived at their destination!*

So – let me paraphrase –

They went to the shore to wait for Jesus.

They got fed up of waiting so.....

They set off  without Him.

They hit a storm and were worried!

Jesus didn't calm the storm this time, as he had done on a

previous occasion,

instead He took them straight to their destination.

How often do we get impatient waiting for Jesus to do something

and head off with our own plan.

Then hit our own storm

and are very relieved when Jesus turns up!

But …… how about ……

being more ready to wait His timing

and avoid some of the unnecessary storms

we bring upon ourselves.

And when we hit the storm we say  -  "Why God?

Why did you let this happen?"

Well that's where our own plans can often take us.

Don't forget what David believed as he wrote in Psalm 37:7

*Be still in the presence of the LORD,*

*and wait patiently for him to act.*

and in verse 23

*The LORD directs the steps of the godly.*

*He delights in every detail of their lives*

David was a man who knew how to wait for God's timing.

Let us be more like David and be patient.

## Let God have His way

We know how parents seek to bring some discipline or control

into a child's life  -  for the greater good of the child.

And we know how grandparents will often undermine them

by pleading on the child's behalf or

slipping the forbidden things to them.

I think in a similar way

people will often - misguidedly - be  like the grandparents

and interfere with what God is doing in someone's life.

They will feed their weaknesses and indulge their sinful nature

out of a desire to help them escape tough situations.

God gives us what we need.

What He knows is best.

He will give us what will refine us

without indulging our sinful nature.

Jesus is the Bread of Life.

The Spirit is the River of Life.

He will meet our hunger - He will satisfy our thirst.

But ……. He will do it in a right way,

whereas people may do it in a wrong way.
They may do it with the best of intentions
but still not the best from God's perspective.

## Ephesians 2:10

*We are created in Christ Jesus*

*to do good works,*

*which God prepared*

*in advance for us to do.*

So .....

Rest in what God is doing.

- - -

Not in what you want to do.

# A spiritual journey

Do you sometimes wonder what your life is all about?

You feel you're carrying something from God.

There's a message in your spirit.

But you don't see it's outworking at the moment.


Consider the possibility ......

Are you walking a spiritual journey

that hasn't yet found

it's physical expression in this place?


Don't despair - as in Hebrews 11

others have walked a similar pathway before

and those who hear the voice of God

will continue to do so in the future

It's the way of the Father for the faithful.


Heb 11:13

All these people were still living by faith when they died.

They did not receive the things promised;

they only saw them and welcomed them from a distance.

And they admitted that they were aliens and strangers on earth.

But they were part of God's eternal purposes.

## Prayer

How do we learn not to pray with our own agenda

but to pray His agenda?

How do we learn to pray His purposes?

Is it more about relationship than issues?

Is it more about getting to know Father .....

rather than raising issues

and requesting the answer

from our perspective?

Is it more about knowing things ....

from His perspective?

I think so.

## In the silence

We sometimes feel that times of silence in our life

Is fruitless and wasted but ....

In the silent times ...... from God's perspective

He is building character He can trust

Interesting !!

So...... don't resist the silence.

Don't fight the silence.

Embrace the silence

and reflect on what God is doing.

## Learn to live in stillness

Learn to live in stillness.

Learn to live in quietness.

Learn to live in calm ..... in your inner being

no matter what is going on around

and you will find

that you will hear the voice of Father

much more easily.

<u>Settling for less than the best</u>

In Numbers 32 and Joshua 22 we see
how 2½ tribes of the Israelites
preferred to stay east of the Jordan
rather than entering the blessing and promises
of the Promised Land.
Settling for what was pleasing to the eye
rather than the fullness of what God wanted to give them.
And many people today have settled
for something less than God's best,
preferring to stay in the safety of the known and the
predictability of life.
Rather than following the call of God
into the new season that He is bringing forth.

## God made Man

Have you ever considered ......

that when God made man

He made him a mixture of

..... dust and deity ......

Which are you more aware of in yourself .....

the dust?

or the deit?

## The Answer is God!

Why are men still searching for the answer?

Why will they not just accept the truth?

That ......

God, Himself .....

is the key to the riddle of the Universe.

They keep searching

but they won't find another answer.

## He doesn't owe us an explanation

God doesn't owe us an explanation

for what He does.

He's sovereign over all.

He owes us nothing.

Yet He has given us everything

if we receive the salvation He has offered.

But don't forget -

He doesn't owe us an explanation

for what He does.

So just thank Him for His grace and mercy

when He does choose to explain.

## Preparing a Place for You

In John 14 Jesus says – *I go to prepare a place for you.*
And in the same way as natural parents prepare
a nursery for their expected child
with loving care and thought applied to every decision
and every detail,
so Jesus is preparing a place for you.
Unlike natural parents
who don't know who they are preparing for
and what will best suit them
Jesus knows each one of us individually.
He knows who He is preparing for
and so the place He prepares is custom-made.
Uniquely planned to suit you exactly.
He knows who you are and what you are like.
And He prepares a place that will delight me
down to the finest details
when I finally enter the spiritual realm.

## The Power of Prayer

Matt 6:10 says -

*Your kingdom come, your will be done on earth*

*as it is in heaven.*

It's through prayer ……

that we bring two worlds together -

God's world and this world.

The spiritual realm and the physical realm.

So that ……

the spiritual world can have an influence or impact

on where we are in this world.

So pray with that in mind.

Pray with that as your focus.

## To see like Jesus

John 1:17 says *For the law was given through Moses;*

*Grace and truth came through Jesus Christ.*

The law says "Do not ……" but grace and truth are different

John 2:10 says

*The man said, "Everyone brings out the choice wine first and*

*then the cheaper wine after the guests have had too much to*

*drink; but you have saved the best till now."*

When the guests were already drunk ……

Jesus gave them more wine!

In the temple courts he found men selling cattle, sheep and

doves, and others sitting at tables exchanging money.

So he made a whip out of cords, and drove all from the temple

It was a church activity which probably benefitted many people

who had no other way of obtaining a sacrifice for their worship.

But …….. Jesus saw something deeper in the greed and

deception that was going on.

Would we close down Church activities today?

Would we refuse to give more wine to those who were already

drunk?

Jesus works from a different basis and we need to connect with

Him

We use the law more than we use grace and truth

## A Channel

A Christian is a channel for the nature of God

A mind through which Christ thinks.

A heart through which Christ loves.

A voice through which Christ speaks.

A hand through which Christ helps.

Are you living as a channel for God?

## The Journey

God doesn't promise a calm passage,

but …….

don't worry!

He is with you all the way

and

You are assured of a safe landing.

## To be used

Do not pray for the Lord to use you,

but pray that He will make you usable.

We so easily say -

Lord ... I want to do this or that.

I want to preach, I want to heal.

Please use me.

But we should better say -

make me usable for what You want to do.

But that means change and we don't want to change.

That means yielding to God's agenda

And giving up my agenda!

Are you willing to be usable in the way that God wants to use you

no matter what?

## A Final Thought

Everything for You Father.

Let everything I do ……

Let everything I say ……

be

For the honour of Your Name

For the increase of Your glory

And for Your Kingdom.

Books & EBooks by John J Sweetman which might interest the Reader

The Emerging Kingdom

Babylon or Jerusalem – Your Choice

The Book of Joshua

The Book of Judges

The Book of Ruth

The Book of 1 Samuel

The Book of 2 Samuel

The Book of 1 Corinthians

The Book of 2 Corinthians

Printed in Great Britain
by Amazon